THE 50 TOUGHEST QUESTIONS
MY CLERGY & COUNSELLING FRIENDS ARE
REGULARLY ASKED

QUESTIONS
&
RESPONSES

— ③ —

ROWLAND CROUCHER

COVENTRY
PRESS

Published in Australia by
Coventry Press
33 Scoresby Road
Bayswater Vic. 3153
Australia

ISBN 9780648566175

Copyright © Rowland Croucher 2020

All rights reserved. Other than for the purposes and subject to the conditions prescribed under the *Copyright Act*, no part of this publication may be reproduced, stored in a retrieval system, or transmitted in any form or by any means, electronic, mechanical, photocopying, recording or otherwise, without the prior permission of the publisher.

Unless otherwise indicated, Scripture quotations are from the *New Revised Standard Version Bible*, copyright 1989, Division of Christian Education of the National Council of the Churches of Christ in the United States of America. Used by permission. All rights reserved.

Scripture taken from *The Message*. Copyright © 1993, 1994, 1995, 1996, 2000, 2001, 2002. Used by permission of NavPress Publishing Group.

Cataloguing-in-Publication entry is available from the National Library of Australia http://catalogue.nla.gov.au/.

Cover by Ian James – www.jgd.com.au
Design by Film Shot Graphics – (FSG)
Typeset in Times

Printed in Australia

CONTENTS

INTRODUCTION

Chapter 1 7
How To Get Along With The People You Live With

Chapter 2 20
Tim Costello

Chapter 3 33
Women (And Men): What The Bible Really Says

Chapter 4 48
Caring For God's Creation: Climate Change And Other Matters

Chapter 5 66
Ken R. Manley

Chapter 6 78
LGBTIS Are Loved By God Too!

Chapter 7 92
Father Rod Bowers: Australia's Best-Known Contemporary Popular Prophet

Chapter 8 99
Dealing With Hate

Chapter 9 111
Creativity And Religious Institutions: A Potpourri Of Wisdom

Chapter 10 123
Richard Rohr: An Appreciation

Chapter 11 133
Growing Old Gracefully

Chapter 12 149
My Hero Caleb

Chapter 13 169
Death And Dying

Postscript ....

INTRODUCTION

Greetings again, questioning friends. This little collection of 'chapters-about-the-big-issues' comprises the third in our series where we attempt to face honestly the stuff which bothers – or excites – people with hungry minds.

What have folks done with these little books? From the feedback I've received, they carry them around to provide food-for-pondering. (You can fit this little tome in your purse or coat-pocket, to read in the bus or train or plane). Pastors borrow ideas-for-preaching here; or they're curricula for small-group or family discussions. Good: feel free to use any of these dozen or so chapters for 'edifying' yourself and others. Trust me: people are worrying/pondering/arguing about these things...

Where do these topics originate? From questions my nearly 5000 friends ask me on Facebook; from letters-to-editors (I read three major newspapers most days); from my own reading (life is actually slowing down for this geriatric approaching my 83rd birthday); and from issues people raise with me in a small counselling ministry...

Again, here we use two chapter models in our quest-for-answers. We have four biographies - a well-known Catholic intellectual (Richard Rohr); an Anglican prophet (Rod Bower) and two amazing peripatetic Australian Baptists (Tim Costello and Ken Manley). In two chapters, we look at basic relationships (how to love and not hate the people we 'do life with'), and another where this 'mere male' attempts to summarise what he's learned in several thousand hours counselling women. We tackle two Big Issues for moderns: Climate Change, and how to relate to LGBTI's.

(Some other complex issues – like why humans suffer from pandemics, why adults, including clergy, abuse children, or why there's so much violence perpetrated against others – even in the name of religion – will have to wait for the next book, or the one after that.)

In one chapter, we all-too-briefly look at churches-as-institutions; in another, we ask how some people grow old gracefully, and others grumpily; and in another, how to face death with serenity and hope.

Sincere thanks to five special people: my very gifted editor Hugh McGinlay; my faithful secretary Kath Timewell; my generous friend Noel Morley (who keeps my computer happy); the Rev. Dr Philip Hughes who's been a faithful chairman of the John Mark Ministries Board for about twenty years; and to my current pastor Rev. Jim Barr, who faithfully models what it truly means to 'serve the Lord with joy'.

Enjoy the ride! Feel free to contact me with comments and suggestions: rcroucher@gmail.com.

Shalom!

Rowland Croucher

Chapter 1
HOW TO GET ALONG WITH THE PEOPLE YOU LIVE WITH

In the brilliant film *Kramer vs Kramer*, the divorced father has to explain to his 5-year-old that he's just lost the custody battle between himself and the boy's mother. Soon the child will be going to live with her. The little boy sobs out what for him are questions of ultimate concern. 'Where will I sleep? Where will I put my toys? Why can't I stay with you too?'

The movie is about three people. Two big people – a man and a woman – have needs that aren't being met by the other. Their little boy, therefore, has to have his life messed up too. Where does such a vicious circle begin? What can we do to stop the chain-reaction of such grief being handed on to another generation?

Human relationships are the target for seminars and sermons, conferences and commissions, newspaper and magazine articles. Best-seller lists tell us how to be human. You can pay hundreds of dollars to learn about Conflict Resolution or Gestalt Therapy or Active Listening or How to be both Gentle and Assertive...

Sex no longer belongs in the bedroom of two people committed for life: it's often a spectator (and very competitive and sometimes fraught) sport. We live further away, on average, from our relatives than ever before. More women are climbing professional ladders than ever before. Families move house more than ever before. In some Western countries, marriage and divorce rates are nearly equal. A Sydney medical specialist tells us, 'If it weren't for tranquillisers, modern civilisation wouldn't be surviving'. Some tensions in living with others are as old as history (e.g. Cain and Abel). We all agree with the Psalmist: 'How wonderful it is, how pleasant, for God's people to live together in harmony' (133:1). And Paul makes sense too: 'Don't quarrel... Be kind to everyone, good, patient, gentle...' (2 Timothy 2:24). But how in a world – or a home – like ours? Someone said of our church: 'It's full of people who've got it all together.' Wrong. Perhaps their disciplined middle-classness was a cover for covert struggles nobody but the counselling staff knew about. Yes, there were some real saints: but for many life was a matter of quiet desperation: like the good man who came to talk – crying almost non-stop for an hour – about his failures with the son he loved...

Sometime our families are nice on the outside, but hellish when the doors are locked.

The Bible is full of such stories. You remember them from Sunday school: Jacob and Esau, Jacob and his sons, Hosea and his wife... And the more genteel family comprising two sisters - Mary and Martha. They related to Jesus very differently, because their instincts differed: Martha was a practical person, and her sister was more 'social', desiring a deep conversation about important matters to do with ultimate realities. When Martha exploded out of the kitchen, I read Jesus' reaction as affirming her: 'Martha, you're anxious about preparing a nice meal. Thanks for that. But what I need now is not food so much as a listening ear, and Mary's giving me that. She's perceived my deeper hunger. Let's make the meal simple - just a cup of soup will do - and come and join our conversation...'

How can we be sensitive to another's need, as Mary was? 'All happy families resemble one another; every unhappy family is unhappy in its own way' said Tolstoy in *Anna Karenina*.

So how can we get along with those we live with? Here are eight suggestions:

1. ACCEPTING your own and others' uniqueness.

Do you like yourself? If you don't, you'll often have trouble relating to others. Sometimes when counseling, I ask 'What do you like about yourself?' and often get the response 'Very little'. My pastoral mentor John Claypool says he's asked scores of people over the years 'Are you gifted?' and rarely does he receive an affirmative answer. Sometimes we cover our deficiencies with 'Well, nobody's perfect!' Of course, of course – and we should be willing to admit that – including parents to their children.

When parents make mistakes, they should apologise. And children should see the biblical modelling of confession and forgiveness in action – in (and between) their parents.

Perhaps the hardest person to forgive is yourself, especially if your parents scolded you too often. If they have unresolved self-esteem issues, they may offload their frustrations on to their children, berating them as 'bad' or 'stupid'. If it happens too often, those children might go right through life believing such negativity. I remember a conversation with someone who'd attempted to take her life. She told me, 'My parents never said anything nice about me. I was born five days after they got married. I wasn't wanted: and they told me constantly I was their #1 problem...'

Maturity is when we've forgiven our parents for being human too. So they didn't understand you. They're not God. They too sometimes 'know in part and see through a glass darkly' as Paul puts it in 1 Corinthians 13:12.

Immature parents or friends may not be able to cope with others' uniqueness and 'difference'. Parents – and preachers – sometimes use their authority to give vent to their own frustrations, especially if 'the other' does or believes something different from their set of doctrines or values. (I have a theory that folks aren't allowed to ask questions in churches often because the pastor is insecure with difference. The more insecure, the more there's a temptation to find heresies everywhere... Fortunately the God I believe in has no needs of his own, and simply encourages us to grow into the unique person we were destined by his grace to become.)

I have some notes of a sermon I preached at Blackburn Baptist Church in the early 1980s which read: 'Please forgive me if ever I scold you or want to change you into my image. I pledge that, to the best of my ability, I will accept you, love you, just as you are. I won't dump hard expectations on to you. If ever as a preacher I get into 'exhortation' mode, please know that I too am part of the 'target audience'...

'Let's study Jesus in all this. Let's study the lives of the "saints" who modelled their behaviour on that of Jesus. That's what the best people in the biblical drama did: they modelled their lives on saints who displayed outstanding faith and hope and love. Read the "roll call" of faithful people in Hebrews 11...'

'So accept yourself. You are an unrepeatable miracle of God's creation. If you want to get along with others, start with the person inside your own skin!'

2. BELONGING to a family/group/community.

Oscar Wilde reckoned 'other people are quite dreadful; the only possible society is oneself'. (Why not Google that quote and discover why he felt like that?)

God's human creatures were not meant to live alone (Genesis 2:18). Paul agrees: 'None of us lives for ourselves only' (Romans 14:7). Frederick Buechner says that humanity is like a spider-web: 'As we move around this world', he observed in *The Hungering Dark*, 'and as we act with kindness, perhaps, or with indifference or with hostility towards the people we meet, we are setting the great spider-web atremble. The life that I touch for good or ill will touch another life, and that in turn another, until who knows where the trembling stops or in what far place my touch will be felt?'

Our influence on others – and theirs on us – is deep and profound. Who I am changes you and who you are changes me. We cannot see all of ourselves by ourselves. Think of it physically: your eyes can see only about 70% of your body. You need a reflector of some sort to see the rest. And so, at a deeper level, your identity, your perception of who you are, has depended upon what others have communicated to you about you! If you think you're Napoleon, or an isosceles triangle, then something's gone terribly wrong with your interpersonal relationships. If you were to move about unseen, unheard, or unnoticed by others then you could begin to doubt your own reality. It's on the esteem of others that we base our self-esteem. We need each other. We are all *dependent*, every moment of our lives, both on God and on others.

Martin Buber realised the importance of this by saying 'the truth is not so much <u>in</u> human beings as *between* them'.

Paul Simon's song says it cynically: 'I've built walls / A fortress deep and mighty / That none may penetrate. I have no need of friendship; / Friendship causes pain. / It's laughter and it's loving I disdain. / I am a rock. I am an island.'

Psychologist Eric Fromm reckoned 'the deepest need of humans is the need to overcome their separateness, to leave the prison of their aloneness...'

As a friend said to me, 'We humans-in-community are more like honeycomb than marbles let loose on the ground...'

The poet Robert Browning practised all this. He literally invited Elizabeth Barrett to live. Elizabeth's mother had died when the eleven Barrett children were young, and her father was a despotic tyrant with the kids. Frail most of her life, Elizabeth eventually became a bed-ridden invalid. The doctor told her she had 'consumption' and she believed him, and was utterly defeated. Being so sick, she got special attention, a room of her own, and freedom from her father's rages...

When she was nearly 40, she met Robert Browning, who fell so madly in love with her that a day or two after their first meeting he wrote her an impassioned love-letter. Overcoming her fears, he swept her out of the sick-room and into marriage, dismissing her symptoms as so many cobwebs. At 41, she traveled extensively; at 43 she bore a perfectly healthy child. For the rest of her life, she wrote wonderful poetry that could only come from a vital person...

We too can be kindlers of life or death in others. We belong together and need each other.

3. COMMUNICATING.

I remember making a resolution to talk to my wife more than to any other individual; and try to spend some time each day communicating with each of my four children. To do this, we tried to spend family-time with dinner-time each night, and told the church a telephone answering machine would take calls during this precious time. The church was most understanding...

One of the great sicknesses of our time is affability, being 'nice'. But in the process we sometimes aren't honest with others, and play games to cover our true feelings. The truly Christian approach is to 'walk in the light as God is in the light' as the Bible exhorts us (1 John 1:7), rather than keeping others in the dark. When we hide the realities of our situations we may become phoney with each other, depriving us of true sharing, *koinonia*.

However, the opposite problem is just as bad, if not worse. We are not invited to share our criticisms when it might cause pain rather than healing. Rarely is a wife helpful when she screams 'And you call yourself a man!' or he says, when her cooking has failed, 'You'll never learn!' Or the parent says to the child, 'Why can't you behave like ...? They wouldn't do that!' Or a teacher greets a brilliant, creative story with criticisms of the child's spelling... Such attitudes are destructive, reinforcing our negative view/s of ourselves. They stifle our confidence, and we feel even more of a failure than we were.

Another form of bad communication is the 'wait until the weekend' or 'the next spare moment' routine. This has the latent message, 'You don't matter very much to me right now. My program matters more than your needs'.

And we need help when we're on the receiving end of this sort of treatment. I tend to write a note about anything I promise someone. But (says he righteously!), I get a bit 'cheesed off' when someone promises something but doesn't write it down. (John Stott used to prompt his staff-members when this happened.) I tend to be rigorous with myself, but I need to be accepting of the different approaches of others. Sometimes that, for me, has been difficult.

An old song says, 'He's alright when you know him, but you've got to know him first'. If your face tonight is grim and miserable, then I'm not going to blame you: I need to know why you're tired/sad/whatever, so that we can talk about it when the moment is right. Behind whatever face you're wearing, you're OK. Parents need to understand not to be threatened by the changing moods of their adolescent children: adolescence is a hard time, both for the kids and their parents. Young people are then looking for their identity; they are pressured to conform to the behaviours/language etc. of their peer group. They're awkward in some contexts. They are dealing with their sexual awakening. All this adds up to a pretty complicated time. So we parents will love our children unconditionally (not 'I will love you if you...' but 'I love you').

4. DECISION-MAKING

How does it happen in your home? According to a survey of happy and unhappy families, the happiest are those that talk things over the most. This survey found that even hostile arguments are better than someone in the home making decisions for the others autocratically. And if these happy families find one person who has better judgment than the others, they give that person the final say after discussion (e.g. about money matters). And it goes without saying we'll always give reasons for our decisions.

Although the New Testament normally gives fathers the ultimate authority in the home, there are also times when the New Testament talks about mutuality in the area of submission. Dads are not supposed to be dictators: they lead by love and a good example. The kids will *know* he loves his wife/their mother. They'll see evidence of it all the time. The best gift a dad can give his children? Loving their mother.

From today's desk calendar: 'Never miss an opportunity to make others happy, even if you have to leave them alone to do it'.

5. DOING for others what they cannot do for themselves.

We exist in our homes for each other. The people I live with aren't there to serve me; I'm to serve them. That's the attitude of followers of the servant-Christ.

Why 'doing' rather than 'caring'? Henri Nouwen points out that the word 'care' has become quite ambiguous. When a mafia leader tells his henchmen to 'go and take care' of somebody, that somebody had better watch out. He is about to be made an offer he can't refuse! Actually, our English word 'care' goes back to a Gothic root, *kara*, which means 'to lament, to weep with, to grieve'. So caring should mean to become aware of the other in ways that stir deep feelings, and out of such feelings a resolve is born to DO for them what we can. This involves breaking out of the circle and making our lives a resource for others...

This is the moral of the Good Samaritan story. Every Good Samaritan says to the one in need: WHAT HAPPENS TO YOU MAKES A DIFFERENCE TO ME. So God makes an unconditional covenant to commit himself to us no matter what happens, to forgive 'seventy times seven' and serve the other even when/if such labours are not returned, or thanked. This is authentic caring. Love is a verb, it is active not merely passive; it's doing, not just feeling.

And such loving will involve praying for that person, as well as forgiving them. It involves sacrificial giving (Luke 6:27-38).

Ever tried to go on hating someone you keep on praying for???

6. ENJOYING the other's company.

One of the problems of television – or smartphones – is that they give us an excuse to be absent when we're present. We've forgotten how to laugh, to sing, and to play together. And to talk together. (A woman told me that when her husband was declared redundant at the age of 40, she found it hard coping with his being at home all day. She said, 'I married him for better and for worse, but not for lunch'!)

Plan some surprises for the people you live with!

7. FEELINGS are neither right nor wrong, they just 'are'.

Carl Sandburg talks about the 'zoo' inside each of us – there's a pig, and a lion, a tiger, and a gentle deer. We have all kinds of feelings within us: we are responsible for some of them and not others. (But although there's a zoo in me, I am the keeper of that zoo!)

For example, it's not wrong to be angry: but what you do with that anger could be sinful (Ephesians 4:26). Jesus got angry sometimes. I should pray for the maturity to handle conflicts constructively. Just as friction between certain types of rocks produces sparks of light, so it is the friction of our individualities rubbing against each other that illuminates who we really are. There is a sense in which I do not really know you nor you me until we get to a point where we differ...

Maybe the words 'ought' and 'should' are inappropriate with regard to feelings. Feelings are like toothache – they're there – and no amount of exhorting will make the toothache, or the feelings, go away. The words 'ought' and 'should' belong more appropriately to the realm of actions.

Now here's the rub: if anybody *really* knew what you were thinking and feeling, what would happen? Two reactions, maybe: the immature might judge, condemn, reject you. But those who are 'in Christ' and have really convinced themselves of his total acceptance of them, might accept you. And of all the places on earth, the Christian community ought to be the place where you'll know you're loved in spite of what you feel about yourself. So why not take off the mask, take some risks with others, and don't expect rejection. But, then, if you are rejected, please know that God accepts you – and that matters more than anything.

I met a woman some time ago who had been very ill. The medication necessary to save her life made her gain enormous amounts of weight. She was huge. Before the illness, she had been very thin and, she thought, pretty. She had been a nurse, a 'success' in the opinion of others. She told me she had to deal with overweight people in her job, and that she had no patience with them. They simply had to exercise more self-control, stop eating so much... 'Sometimes they would cry. They said they couldn't stop eating, or that they did stop eating but didn't lose weight'. She would scold them then, and tell them they were just feeling sorry for themselves. All they had to do was to try harder and presto! they would be thin like her.

She said to me, 'How could I have treated them like that?' I think she wanted to go back to every one of those overweight people and tell them that now she understands; now she knows what it's like. Now she knows how it feels to have people look at you as if you're a failure because you're not what most women in our society are supposed to be – thin and pretty and healthy. This failure taught her compassion, surely one of the most important lessons we can learn. One problem with 'success' is that it's sometimes not a very good teacher of compassion...

When you really get in touch with your own feelings, you'll be more compassionate with others. Here's Frederick Buechner's definition of compassion: 'The sometimes fatal capacity for feeling what it's like to live inside somebody else's skin. It is the knowledge that there can never really be any peace for me until there is peace and joy finally for you too'.

8. AND IN THE END, GOD.

When Jesus was baptised, God's voice from heaven said, 'I love you, my son. I take delight in you'. From that strong affirmation, Jesus was able to resist the temptations that soon came to him. From such a gift of esteem from God, Jesus did not require the approval of others which would have seduced him. Jesus didn't wear masks. He was just who he was. And he's promised to reproduce his character in our lives. He's inviting us to lay aside the 'works of darkness' and walk in the light - with God and with others. He'll give us his unique courage and hope and daring in our relationships. You won't have to vacillate any more between proving you're somebody of worth and value or insisting you're a nobody. You won't have to attract attention – to be loved or hated. Out of the overflow of God's acceptance of you, and your acceptance of that acceptance, you'll get along with others – even those who live with you, and who know you 'warts and all'.

'If you have the why, you'll know the how.' (Nietzsche).

Chapter 2
TIM COSTELLO

According to *Wikipedia*, Tim Costello was born on 4 March 1955; my birth-date (also mentioned by *Wikipedia*) was in 1937. Our journeys into Christian ministry – and through life – are oddly similar.

We both had somewhat conservative fathers – each known for resisting new theological ideas. Both were advocates/practitioners of physical discipline ('Spare the rod and spoil the child'). And in terms of their vocations, neither was interested in being promoted: Tim's dad was a classroom teacher all his working life; my 'public servant' father moved paper across a desk most of his working years. Tim's dad had a very high IQ (according to his wife, Tim's mother Anne, who first met him at the University of Melbourne as she was psychologically testing fellow-students, Russell was in the 'genius' category.)

Tim and I were the eldest sons. He had one brother (Peter) and a sister (Janet). I have two brothers, no sisters. We were all regular attenders at Sunday school (I at a Brethren Assembly in Sydney; Tim at Blackburn Baptist Church, Melbourne).

Schooling for each of us was very privileged: Tim at Carey Baptist Grammar in Melbourne; I at Sydney Boys High. He then went to Monash University to study law, and did very well. I wandered around the University of Sydney for a couple of years, and did poorly. I then took myself to Bathurst Teachers College and, fortunately, did very well there (top male student; president of the Christian Fellowship, athletics blue, etc.).

Eventually we both increased the 'letters after our names': Tim graduated with a Bachelor of Jurisprudence degree in 1976, a Bachelor of Laws in 1978 and a Diploma of Education in 1979. Later, at the Baptist Seminary in Ruschlikon, Switzerland, he earned a Bachelor of Divinity; and then a Master of Divinity at Whitley College, the Baptist seminary affiliated with the University of Melbourne. He received the Victorian of the Year award in July 2004 in recognition of his public and community service. He was made an officer of the Order of Australia in June 2005 and was the Victorian nominee for the Australian of the Year award in 2006. He was the 2008 winner of the Australian Peace Prize awarded by the Peace Organisation of Australia. He is also listed by the National Trust as a "National Living Treasure". In 2008, Tim Costello received an honorary doctorate from the Australian Catholic University in recognition of 'his contributions to religious life and social justice'. (You'll find my academic degrees in *Wikipedia* if you have nothing better to do!)

Without doubt, Tim's now the best-known and most-listened-to Christian pastor/prophet in Australia.

I reckon/hope that his latest book, *A Lot with a Little*, will be a best-seller. The opening chapter is about Russell's – his dad's – funeral. I was there, and noted the rows of serious-looking Carey Grammar staff in the packed Crossway Church.

Russell had been a 'chocolate soldier' in World War II. Like many others when the war ended, he matriculated, then attended lectures at the evangelical Melbourne Bible Institute, where he got a thorough education in Bible and classical Greek (which he taught there for many years, on top of his job as a schoolteacher). Tim writes, 'My father had found his life's purpose. He was committed at the very core of his being to following Christ'.

This is where I enter the picture. I'd responded to a call from the church Russell and Anne and their three children faithfully attended: Blackburn Baptist Church. It was in the middle of Melbourne's Bible Belt. (Years later as he introduced me as a visiting speaker to a World Vision Staff meeting, Tim said, 'It was actually the "buckle" of the Bible Belt!')

I'd noted Russell's special gift as a 'pastoral networker' and invited him to become an elder. Which he did, after applying to become a member of the church. (Russell wasn't enamoured much with institutional churches, and though previously baptised had never actually joined the church-as-institution).

One night I phoned him from a nearby hospital about 10 p.m: 'Russell, I have a request: would you mind phoning the other elders, and drawing up a roster for them to come on the hour through the night: a lady is dying, and her middle-aged daughter needs some pastoral encouragement'. The patient did pass away about 4 a.m. and the elder-on-duty was Ted Dufty. From then on Ted's face lit up as he told all-and-sundry: 'That was the most amazing experience of my life: we three held hands and I prayed and we said the Lord's Prayer, and I still think of that experience as an elder with deep gratitude'.

[Footnote to that story: why do most pastors deprive their fellow-ministers-in-the-pews from sharing these precious moments? For more, see the three chapters 'The Marks of a Healthy Church' in the second book in this series.]

Margaret Anne, Tim's mother, attended a Presbyterian Church in her childhood, and did well at St. Michael's Church of England School. She – a nonconformist – got the top award for Divinity. At University she gravitated to the Student Christian Movement (SCM), and enjoyed its more liberal emphases on social and political issues. (Chapter 3 in Tim's book is about their courtship; I won't spoil it for you. Tim calls it an 'unlikely union which lasted for sixty-three years, until my father passed away in 2016').

Tim's childhood at Blackburn was, he writes, idyllic. Football was their family's 'surrogate secular religion'. Sundays were church-filled: morning worship, afternoon Christian Endeavour, evenings – when they were old enough – back to church for the PM service. Tim was baptised (by immersion of course!) when he was 15.

Tim's years at Monash University opened his eyes to many dimensions of truth-seeking. He was fascinated by communists, Jews, Indigenous students and others. And he also mentions his appreciation of the care we showed at Blackburn Baptist Church to young people sleeping rough, and women victims of domestic violence. (In fact, our research told us that a woman and a young person wandered the streets every night in that privileged middle-class suburb as a result of domestic violence. My wife Jan's aunt left the church a wonderful gift of her house in Box Hill, which has been used to shelter 'battered women' for decades now.)

Peter went to Monash two years after Tim, and was famously active in student politics. Tim was busy with his leadership responsibilities as president of the Evangelical Union. Merridie, who was eventually to become Tim's wife, also started studying for her teaching career – via an Arts degree at Monash – a year after Tim. (I'll let you enjoy the pages on courtship and marriage!)

Following Monash was the beginning of a career practising law, becoming director of Prison Fellowship, and ministering to a thriving youth group of up to 45 people. But within a short time, Tim felt called to seriously study theology, so in 1980 he and Merridie found themselves en route to the Baptist Seminary in Ruschlikon, Switzerland. There, they were 'tossed into the deep end', doing courses in New Testament Greek, Hebrew, a semester of Latin, as well as the normal streams of New Testament, Old Testament, church history, pastoral care and mission. An interesting lesson-in-humility for Tim involved Merridie's achieving a high distinction in one of their early units! He also accepted a pastoral ministry in a small multi-cultural church for a day a week. [1]

Questions Tim faced in seminary included these: 'Are faith and the Bible relevant to foreign policy, war, refugees and economics? Was the Bible to be taken seriously in its message of love for enemies, embrace of the stranger or refugee? On what basis do we pick and choose, and by what criteria do we invoke higher norms for policy other than our belief in the word of God? If not applicable to economics, refugees, poverty or defence, then why follow its prohibition on homosexuality to oppose same sex marriage?' Good questions, Tim! Two of the scholars Tim particularly focused on were John Howard Yoder and Reinhold Niebuhr.

After Ruschlikon, on an interesting holiday trip through the U.S. with his wife and parents, Tim (now somewhat more progressive theologically) and his theologically conservative father had some dynamic discussions on this and that. They discovered that many American evangelicals didn't like Jimmy Carter's social conscience, and his talk about human rights in international relations. The Christian conservative movement 'Moral Majority' actually backed Reagan over Carter; 'They backed a divorced non-Church attending, pro-low taxes for the rich, anti-communist in Reagan to arrest the USA's moral decay. (The same group a generation later voted en masse for a thrice-divorced failed casino magnate who fathered five children with three women and boasted of his sexual assaults on women – an immediate disqualification of a candidate in any other democracy).' [2] Tim goes on to explain: 'Dad's charity stopped short of justice... Camara said "When I feed the poor, they call me a saint. When I ask why they are poor, they call me a Communist."'

And while in the U.S., 'we were hit by... headlines announcing that the Southern Baptists... had banned women from ever preaching or being ordained. Why? Because Eve had sinned first and led Adam astray'. [3]

ooOoo

An easy-read interview with Tim was published in 2018 by Roland Ashby in *A Faith to Live By* [4]. Here are a few quotes (some wisdom from Tim on matters he doesn't mention in his later book, I think):

How did you hold on to your faith when witnessing the terrible scenes following a tsunami? 'Curiously, the tsunami strengthened my faith… the resource of faith was all the people who were victims of the tsunami had to appeal to. In Sri Lanka this is Muslim and Buddhist faith, not just Christian faith. One man said "If I couldn't believe in God, I couldn't get out of bed and try again. I've lost my family, I've lost my home. That's all I've got".' [5]

'I don't think there is any intellectual or theological answer to theodicy (the problem of evil and suffering), other than [that]… God has entered our suffering, taken death into himself in Jesus, embraced betrayal, unfair trial, torture, death and profound injustice… I believe God… in Jesus, is no stranger to this.'

'I was profoundly moved seeing Israeli Arabs and Israeli Jews sit and talk about the same loss. The common bond was grief; they had lost children. Arab parents had lost children to the Israeli defence forces, Jewish parents had lost children to the Shaheed suicide bombers…' [6]

'I sign all my letters with the [powerful Jewish] greeting of peace, Shalom – [which] is a word that means a right ordering in relationships: let there be shalom in your marriage, in your business dealings, in your courts…'

'We are witnessing a toxic political rhetoric on the federal level... Bob Katter talks of... Curtin and Chifley who lived in much worse times, who would never had made the sort of personal attacks that we see now.' [7]

'I have a prayer room in our house, where I write my diary each day. When I find it hard to pray, I write. I find it easier to pray when I'm jogging.' [8]

'Catherine Hamlin [is] an Aussie saint, one of the early women at Sydney University to do medicine, could have had a fantastic career teaching surgery here, but chose to bury herself in Ethiopia with the most despised, women with fistula. And when you meet her, you feel here is a person who has missed all the cynicism and shallowness of our culture because she has been so focused...'

'Why do I like George W. Bush? He gave the largest increase in overseas aid, far greater than Clinton or Obama or others, and this is a story not known. The Prepfar (President's Emergency Relief for AIDS Relief) Funds were a George Bush initiative. [9]

ooOoo

And now back to Tim's new book for more experiences/insights.

During the trip through the U.S. Tim's dad asked him why would he ever accept a call to be the pastor of Melbourne's St Kilda Baptist Church – a small congregation with fewer than sixteen members? Chapter 12 has some inspiring stories about people 'at the bottom of the heap' who found faith and Christian love during Tim's years there. He combined his legal practice with his pastoring; developed some progressive ideas about the social housing; and how to be a Christian local councillor – and Lord Mayor (he was elected to his own astonishment, and to Merridie's chagrin). His text at his installation as Lord Mayor was from Isaiah 65: 'The poor shall build houses and live in them'. During these years, he also found himself accepting the arguments for the legalisation of prostitution...

And during this time, he had a surprising visit from two Federal politicians – members of the Australian Democrats – inviting him to stand for Federal parliament. It didn't eventuate, but was tempting, and it's all an interesting story I won't spoil for you...

Tim's next appointment was a call to Collins Street Baptist Church, where with his co-minister Rev. Jim Barr he began various ministries to feed and house homeless people in the inner city. [10]

One of his initiatives (in 1995) was the formation of the Interchurch Gambling Taskforce. The major political parties did virtually nothing to help problem gamblers. Tim is still a well-known spokesman for gambling reform. 'The 1999 productivity commission confirmed the shocking news that Australia, with 0.2% of the world's population, had 20% of all the world's poker machines... Now times have changed. Every opinion survey shows that over 70% of the public wants pokies gone altogether.' 'When pokies were introduced women were only 7% of the problem gambling population, but later that figure jumped to over 50%' [11].

Tim's next ministry was as CEO of World Vision (from 2004). His first visit to a disaster-zone was to Darfur in Sudan – an area the size of France with a massive refugee population of women and children in untold suffering. Then the Indian Ocean tsunami on Boxing Day saw Tim cancelling part of his holidays to fly to Sri Lanka: he got to Colombo within 48 hours of the disaster. 'The total deaths across seven nations was nearly 300,000 people... The Australian Prime Minister John Howard pledged $1billion to Indonesia...' [12]

Tim had many jousts with politicians about foreign aid. Here's an interesting paragraph [13]: 'Have a read of Prime Minister Scott Morrison's maiden speech in 2008. It was about the 6500 people who die every day in Africa from preventable and treatable diseases. He said of Africa: "When the history books are written, our age will be remembered for... what we did – or did not do..." He commended the Howard Government's increased spending on foreign aid and said, "However, we must go further because the need is not diminishing nor can our support. It is the Australian thing to do..." 'He later sat in the Abbott Cabinet that withdrew virtually all Australian aid to Africa, and later, as treasurer, slashed aid.' [14]

One of the side-benefits of being a 'high flying celebrity' gets Tim to participate in all sorts of public events. At a TV 'MasterChef' event, the Dalai Lama said he liked every dish: '[As a Buddhist] whatever we are given, when we go from house to house with our food bowls, we eat with thanksgiving. We do not judge.' Tim writes: 'I could see the main comperes looking at each other with slight panic. I could sense their show going down the gurgler... In jest, to alleviate the tension, I said, "As a Christian, I am into judgment. Now this is what I liked...'

[15]
Well, there are so many awful and beautiful stories in the remainder of Tim's book. Some moving headlines:

* 'The Syrian civil war has killed over 600,000 and displaced 12 million Syrians'.

* 'I am pro Israel's right to exist. But our work in the West Bank and Gaza has also convinced me of the Palestinian right to exist'.

* 'Development is three things: keeping children under five alive; educating them, and then finding them a job... [Worldwide] the dollars spent on aid don't amount to more than twenty dollars per person per year'.

* 'Two million South Sudanese have fled, and over one million of these have moved into Uganda. I cannot praise the Ugandan Government enough for refusing to close the border'.

* 'One million Rohingya have fled Myanmar's shocking ethnic cleansing... [Why do] intelligent Burmese people become irrational and visceral in their hatred towards the Rohingya, a group so discriminated against that it is illegal to even utter the word "Rohingya" there, although Rohingya have been there for centuries'.

* 'Australian PM Tony Abbott, in September 2015, agreed to a one-off intake of 12,000 Syrian refugees… Canadians [on the other hand] for the past few years have absorbed annually 17,000 refugees through private sponsorship in addition to their normal government humanitarian intake… The Canadian prime minister, Justin Trudeau, stood at the airport welcoming refugees to cheering crowds'.

* Finally: 'I am neither right nor left, not even centre… I find myself wanting to go neither left nor right nor centre, but to go deeper.'

Amen!

Bibliography

Tim Costello: *A Lot with a Little*, Hardie Grant Books (Melbourne), 2019.

Roland Ashby, *A faith to live by*, Morning Star Publishing, 2018 (chapter on Tim Costello, 'An activist for Gospel justice', pp. 113ff).

Google Philip Adams (ABC Radio National) for a 53 minute interview with Tim, September 2019.

Endnotes

[1] I got a letter or two from Tim during his time in Switzerland asking if I was interested in taking on a

pastoral or chaplaincy position. I forget the details, but reluctantly had to decline the offer.

[2] p. 121.

[3] p.125.

[4] Roland Ashby in *A Faith to Live By*, pp. 113 ff.

[5] Op. cit. p. 113.

[6] Ibid. p. 114.

[7] Ibid. p. 115.

[8] Ibid. p. 116.

[9] Ibid p. 117. Catherine Hamlin died in 2020.

[10] Our daughter Lindy worked with Urban Seed and lived in a flat at the back of Collins Street Baptist Church during some of these years.

[11] p. 190.

[12] p. 229.

[13] p. 243.

[14] Ibid.

[15] p. 254.

Chapter 3
WOMEN (AND MEN):
WHAT THE BIBLE REALLY SAYS

We are entering very complex / important territory in this chapter...

I grew up in a very conservative church which was strong about the notion of male 'headship'. Only men spoke in the public gatherings. Yes, in Ephesians 5:23, Paul writes about the husband being 'the head of the wife' but goes on to talk about the husband giving himself in service for his wife even to the point of giving his life for her. It's costly 'headship'. Then note that Paul affirmed the practice of women praying, and communicating to churches in public (1 Corinthians 11:5). He commends Nymphia who led a house church (1 Corinthians 4:15), and greets Junia a woman apostle (Romans 16:7). (Apostles were people who were 'first in the church'. More on all that later...)

As I write, in today's newspaper there's a story about an Australian Catholic Archbishop who disendorsed an outspoken nun – Sister Joan Chittister – from speaking at a National Catholic Education Conference. Why? She had repeatedly called for the empowerment of women and laypeople in the Catholic Church. [1]

Our Catholic friends, of course, are continuing an approach to sexism that goes way back into history. Let's not forget our own history here: for example, back in the 1800s, in the Victorian age, women lived not under glass ceilings as professional women might put it, but in glass prisons. During the reign of Queen Victoria, women did not have the right to vote, sue or own property. When they married, Victorian wives became the property of their husbands, giving them rights to what their bodies produced: children, sex and domestic labour. The husband controlled all property, earnings and money. If husbands had affairs with other women, wives had simply to endure the infidelity, as they had no rights to divorce on these grounds. And mothers had no right to access their children after divorce...

The earliest stirrings of suffragism can be traced to Victoria's reign: in 1872 the American suffragette Susan B. Anthony was knocked to the ground and arrested for the crime of voting in New York...

Now why is the empowerment of women still such a problem in most cultures and many branches of the Christian church?

Let's begin with a short piece by my fellow Baptist, and the world's most famous 'lay Bible teacher', ex-President Jimmy Carter:

'Women and girls have been discriminated against for too long in a twisted interpretation of the Word of God.

'I have been a practising Christian all my life and a deacon and Bible teacher for many years. My faith is a source of strength and comfort to me, as religious beliefs are to hundreds of millions of people around the world. So my decision to sever my ties with the Southern Baptist Convention, after six decades, was painful and difficult. It was, however, an unavoidable decision when the convention's leaders, quoting a few carefully selected Bible verses and claiming that Eve was created second to Adam and was responsible for original sin, ordained that women must be "subservient" to their husbands and prohibited from serving as deacons, pastors or chaplains in the military service.

'This view that women are somehow inferior to men is not restricted to one religion or belief. Women are prevented from playing a full and equal role in many faiths. Nor, tragically, does its influence stop at the walls of the church, mosque, synagogue or temple. This discrimination, unjustifiably attributed to a Higher Authority, has provided a reason or excuse for the deprivation of women's equal rights across the world for centuries.

'At its most repugnant, the belief that women must be subjugated to the wishes of men excuses slavery, violence, forced prostitution, genital mutilation and national laws that omit rape as a crime. But it also costs many millions of girls and women control over their own bodies and lives, and continues to deny them fair access to education, health, employment and influence within their own communities.

'The impact of these religious beliefs help explain why in many countries boys are educated before girls; why girls are told when and whom they must marry; and why many face enormous and unacceptable risks in pregnancy and childbirth because their basic health needs are not met.

'In some Islamic nations, women are restricted in their movements, punished for permitting the exposure of an arm or ankle, deprived of education, prohibited from driving a car or competing with men for a job. If a woman is raped, she is often most severely punished as the guilty party in the crime.

'The same discriminatory thinking lies behind the continuing gender gap in salaries... It is not women and girls alone who suffer. It damages all of us. The evidence shows that investing in women and girls delivers major benefits for society. An educated woman has healthier children. She is more likely to send them to school. She earns more and invests what she earns in her family.

'It is simply self-defeating for any community to discriminate against half its population. We need to challenge these self-serving and outdated attitudes and practices – as we are seeing in Iran where women are at the forefront of the battle for democracy and freedom.

'I understand, however, why many political leaders can be reluctant about stepping into this minefield. Religion, and tradition, are powerful and sensitive areas to challenge. But my fellow elders and I, who come from many faiths and backgrounds, no longer need to worry about winning votes or avoiding controversy – and we are deeply committed to challenging injustice wherever we see it. The Elders are an independent group of eminent global leaders, brought together by former South African president Nelson Mandela, who offer their influence and experience to support peace building, help address major causes of human suffering and promote the shared interests of humanity. We have decided to draw particular attention to the responsibility of religious and traditional leaders in ensuring equality and human rights and have recently published a statement that declares: "The justification of discrimination against women and girls on grounds of religion or tradition, as if it were prescribed by a Higher Authority, is unacceptable. We are calling on all leaders to challenge and change the harmful teachings and practices, no matter how ingrained, which justify discrimination against women. We ask, in particular, that leaders of all religions have the courage to acknowledge and emphasise the positive messages of dignity and equality that all the world's major faiths share."

'The carefully selected verses found in the Holy Scriptures to justify the superiority of men owe more to time and place – and the determination of male leaders to hold onto their influence – than eternal truths. Similar biblical excerpts could be found to support the approval of slavery and the timid acquiescence to oppressive rulers.

'I am also familiar with vivid descriptions in the same Scriptures in which women are revered as pre-eminent leaders. During the years of the early Christian church, women served as deacons, priests, bishops, apostles, teachers and prophets. It wasn't until the fourth century that dominant Christian leaders, all men, twisted and distorted Holy Scriptures to perpetuate their ascendant positions within the religious hierarchy.' [2]

ooOoo

This esteemed Baptist elder has made his point well. Except for one thing: he doesn't wrestle with the difficult passages in the Christian Bible about the subject. Let's do that now. In a paper read to a Symposium, 'Men, Women and the Church', Dr N.

T. Wright, perhaps the world's leading contemporary English-speaking Evangelical theologian, made these points, among others [3]:

'To infer that women cannot exercise... some kinds of ministry, within the church, is... a shame...

'The New Testament text which is central [to all this] is Galatians 3:28. God has one family, not two, and this family consists of all those who believe in Jesus.

'What Paul says is that there is neither Jew nor Greek, neither slave nor free, no "male and female". I think the reason he says "no male and female" rather than "neither male nor female" is that he is actually quoting Genesis 1, and that we should understand the phrase "male and female" in scare quotes. [4]

More from Tom Wright

'Remember the synagogue prayer in which the man who prays thanks God that he has not made him a Gentile, a slave or a woman? Paul is deliberately marking out the family of Abraham reformed in the Messiah as a people cannot pray that prayer, since within this family these distinctions are now irrelevant.

'Women came first to the tomb, the first to see the risen Jesus, and are the first to be entrusted with the news that he has been raised from the dead... Mary Magdalene and the others are the apostles to the apostles.

'Mary sat at Jesus' feet within the male part of the house rather than being kept in the back rooms with the other women...As is clear from the use of the phrase elsewhere in the NT (for instance, Paul with Gamaliel), to sit at the teacher's feet is a way of saying you are being a student, picking up the teacher's wisdom and learning; and in that very practical world you wouldn't do this just for the sake of informing your own mind and heart, but in order to be a teacher, a rabbi, yourself.

'Saul of Tarsus went to Damascus to catch women and men alike and haul them off into prison. Ken Bailey points out on the basis of his cultural parallels that this only makes sense if the women, too, are seen as leaders, influential figures within the community.

'Ken Bailey says it was taken for granted that men and women would sit apart in church, as still happens today in some circles. Equally important, the service would be held (in Lebanon, say, or Syria, or Egypt), in formal or classical Arabic, which the men would all know but which many of the women would not, since the women would only speak a local dialect or patois. Result? During the sermon in particular, the women, not understanding what was going on, would begin to get bored and talk among themselves.

'As Bailey describes the scene in such a church, the level of talking from the women's side would steadily rise in volume, until the minister would have to say loudly, 'Will the women please be quiet!' What the passage cannot possibly mean is that women had no part in leading public worship, speaking out loud, of course, as they did so. This is the positive point that is proved at once by the other relevant Corinthian passage, 1 Corinthians 11:2–11, since there Paul is giving instructions for how women are to be dressed while engaging in such activities, instruction which obviously would not be necessary if they had been silent in church all the time.

'Didn't Paul himself teach that there was "no male and female, because you are all one in the Messiah" (Galatians 3.28)? Perhaps, indeed, that was one of the "traditions" that he had taught the Corinthian church, who needed to know that Jew and Greek, slave and free, male and female were all equally welcome, equally valued, in the renewed people of God. Perhaps some of the Corinthian women had been taking him literally, so that when they prayed or prophesied aloud in church meetings (which Paul assumes they will do regularly; this tells us, as we've seen, something about how to understand 1 Corinthians 14:34–35) they had decided to remove their normal head-covering, perhaps also unbraiding their hair, to show that in the Messiah they were free from the normal social conventions by which men and women were distinguished.

'The hardest passage of all? 1 Timothy 2. This passage, far and away above all others, has been the sheet-anchor for those who want to deny women a place in the ordained ministry of the church... Women mustn't be teachers, the verse seems to say; they mustn't hold any authority over men; they must keep silent. The whole passage seems to be saying that women are second-class citizens at every level. They aren't even allowed to dress prettily. They are the daughters of Eve, and she was the original troublemaker. The best thing for them to do is to get on and have children, and to behave themselves and keep quiet.

'When you look at strip cartoons, 'B' grade movies, and 'Z' grade novels and poems, you pick up a standard view of how 'everyone imagines' men and women behave. Men are macho, loud-mouthed, arrogant thugs, always fighting and wanting their own way. Women are simpering, empty-headed creatures, with nothing to think about except clothes and jewellery. There are 'Christian' versions of this, too: the men must make the decisions, run the show, always be in the lead, telling everyone what to do; women must stay at home and bring up the children. If you start looking for a biblical back-up for this view, well, what about Genesis 3? Adam would never have sinned if Eve hadn't given in first. Eve has her punishment, and it's pain in childbearing (Genesis 3:16).

'This passage recognises that women, too, should be allowed to study and learn, and should not be restrained from doing so (verse 11). They are to be 'in full submission'; this is often taken to mean 'to the men', or 'to their husbands', but it is equally likely that it refers to their attitude, as learners, of submission to God or to the gospel – which of course would be true for men as well. Then the crucial verse 12 need not be read as 'I do not allow a woman to teach or hold authority over a man' – the translation which has caused so much difficulty in recent years. It can equally mean (and in context this makes much more sense): "I don't mean to imply that I'm now setting up women as the new authority over men in the same way that previously men held authority over women".

'Why might Paul need to say this? There are some signs in the letter that it was originally sent to Timothy while he was in Ephesus. And one of the main things we know about religion in Ephesus is that the main religion – the biggest Temple, the most famous shrine – was a female-only cult. The Temple of Artemis (that's her Greek name; the Romans called her Diana) was a massive structure that dominated the area; and, as befitted worshippers of a female deity, the priests were all women. They ruled the show and kept the men in their place.

'Now if you were writing a letter to someone in a small, new religious movement with a base in Ephesus, and wanted to say that because of the gospel of Jesus the old ways of organising male and female roles had to be rethought from top to bottom, with one feature of that being that the women were to be encouraged to study and learn and take a leadership role, you might well want to avoid giving the wrong impression. Was the apostle saying, people might wonder, that women should be trained up so that Christianity would gradually become a cult like that of Artemis, where women did the leading and kept the men in line? That, it seems to me, is what verse 12 is denying. The word I've translated "try to dictate to them" is unusual, but seems to have the overtones of "being bossy" or "seizing control". Paul is saying, like Jesus in Luke 10, that women must have the space and leisure to study and learn in their own way, not in order that they may muscle in and take over the leadership as in the Artemis-cult, but so that men and women alike can develop whatever gifts of learning, teaching and leadership God is giving them.

'What's the point of the other bits of the passage, then? Why then does Paul finish off with the explanation about Adam and Eve? Remember that his basic point is to insist that women, too, must be allowed to learn and study as Christians, and not be kept in unlettered, uneducated boredom and drudgery. Well, the story of Adam and Eve makes the point well: look what happened when Eve was deceived. Women need to learn just as much as men do. Adam, after all, sinned quite deliberately; he knew what he was doing, and that it was wrong, and went ahead deliberately. The Old Testament is very stern about that kind of action.

'And what about the bit about childbirth? Paul doesn't see it as a punishment. Rather, he offers an assurance that, though childbirth is indeed difficult, painful and dangerous, often the most testing moment in a woman's life, this is not a curse which must be taken as a sign of God's displeasure. God's salvation is promised to all, women and men, who follow Jesus in faith, love, holiness and prudence. And that salvation is promised to those who contribute to God's creation through childbearing, just as it is to everyone else. Let's read this text as I believe it was intended, as a way of building up God's church, men and women, women and men alike.

'How then would I translate the passage? "So this is what I want: the men should pray in every place, lifting up holy hands, with no anger or disputing. In the same way, the women, too, should clothe themselves in an appropriate manner, modestly and sensibly. They should not go in for elaborate hairstyles, or gold, or pearls, or expensive clothes; instead, as is appropriate for women who profess to be godly, they should adorn themselves with good works. They must be allowed to study undisturbed, in full submission to God. I'm not saying that women should teach men, or try to dictate to them; they should be left undisturbed. Adam was created first, you see, and then Eve; and Adam was not deceived, but the woman was deceived, and fell into trespass. She will, however, be kept safe through the process of childbirth, if she continues in faith, love and holiness with prudence."

Tom Wright's Conclusion: 'I believe we have seriously misread the relevant passages in the New Testament, no doubt not least through a long process of assumption, tradition, and all kinds of post-biblical and sub-biblical attitudes that have crept in to Christianity. We need radically to change our traditional pictures both of what men and women are and how they relate to one another within the church and indeed of what the Bible says on this subject.'

ooOoo

A few more jottings

Around one in four Australian women have experienced violence at the hands of a partner or former partner.

Equality doesn't happen by accident. Let us be committed to national movements which address the following:

- Equality in pay, in opportunity, in leadership. health and well-being and in freedom from violence.

- Many Aboriginal women experience the double discrimination of both race and gender.

- Women, on average, retire with 40 per cent less superannuation than men. Why not pay superannuation on Paid Parental Leave?

- *Women and sexual harassment.* In an interesting article in the *Age* newspaper, Stephanie Copus-Campbell, a successful energy industry executive, board member and gender equality advocate writes:

'My first experience of sexual harassment was as a teenager, when the father I was babysitting for wanted to show me his "magazine" collection. I declined and lost my job.

'The next occurred when I was at university and working for a well-known journalist. For weeks, I did my best to ignore his comments... But when words became actions, and he touched me inappropriately, I walked away from a coveted and very much-needed job.

'And it happened three times in my career with the Australian Public Service, including in senior management roles.

In each instance, I ducked, I weaved, and I felt bad. I believed that making a "fuss" would bring negative repercussions — for me.

'Other challenges came with having children. I can remember applying for a secondment at Parliament House, only to be informed (by a woman) that the hours would not be suitable for a mum with young kids. I didn't challenge this explanation. My strongest emotions at missing out on the job were relief and maternal guilt — why indeed was I choosing long hours at work over tucking my kids into bed at night?' [5]

ooOoo

And finally... An elderly lady and her garrulous son attended the church prayer meeting from time to time.

Wal got on his hobby horse one night about women being silent in church and not teaching men.

His mother let him rant for a while, then told him, "God could speak through a donkey, and if he can do that, he can speak through a woman. So shut up, Wal: you are talking nonsense."

God did, and Wal did.

Endnotes

[1] *Sunday Age,* 28 July 2019, p. 3.

[2] *Losing my religion for equality* by Jimmy Carter (president of the United States from 1977 to 1981).

[3] 'Women's Service in the Church: The Biblical Basis', St John's College, Durham, 4 September 2004 by the Bishop of Durham, Dr N. T. Wright.

[4] Note Brethren New Testament scholar F. F. Bruce's comment here: 'Galatians 3:28 is the lens through which we see all of Paul's ideas in this broad area…'

[5] Stephanie Copus-Campbell, an energy industry executive, board member and gender equality advocate. *The Age*, Melbourne, 22 July 2019, p. 22.

Chapter 4
CARING FOR GOD'S CREATION: CLIMATE CHANGE AND OTHER MATTERS

'Rowland, is it OK to call someone a "climate sceptic or denier"'? In my view, no. True skeptics are immersed in scientific inquiry or research, while the word "denier" has connotations of denying tragedies like the Holocaust. Perhaps we should be nice, and use a term like "climate-change doubters" eh? [1]

A potpourri of expert comments

'Entire ecosystems are under threat due to warming oceans, with parts of the Australian coast stretching from Sydney to Adelaide experiencing the most stress, experts warn. Eight of the 10 warmest years of sea surface temperatures have been recorded since 2010 contributing to coral bleaching, oceans acidifying and altering the habitats of different species, a joint study by the Bureau of Meteorology and CSIRO has found.' [2]

In the press late in 2018, (after the announcement about Wentworth voters punishing the government on energy policy), Chief Scientist Alan Finkel said climate change was important for everyday Australians... He 'called on Australia to build a multi-billion hydrogen industry. He said hydrogen, which was close to a zero-emissions fuel, could be Australia's next multi-billion-dollar export opportunity.' [3]

'The past four years were the hottest since global temperature records began, the UN reports in an analysis it says is a "clear sign of continuing long-term climate change". The

UN's World Meteorological Organisation said in November 2019 that 2018 was set to be the fourth warmest year in recorded history, stressing the urgent need for action to rein in runaway planetary warming.' [4]

Another report: 'Himalayan glaciers will shrink by at least a third by the end of the century because of climate change, threatening the livelihoods of millions of people in the mountains and river valleys below, a study has found. The thaw will alter the flow of 10 rivers... causing increased flooding of farmland...' [5]

And in a letter to a newspaper editor: 'As a country renowned for innovation, Germany is planning to phase out coal-generated power stations. This is in stark contrast to the Morrison government, which plans to subsidise the building of more.' [6]

Another: 'Climatologists worry that, in a rapidly warming world, our trees are experiencing unprecedented heat stress... A 2017 study of 1.5 million trees in 29 council areas from Darwin to Launceston, Brisbane to Perth, revealed that nearly one in four trees in urban centres will be at high risk of dieback: wilting, browning of leaves and dead branches...' [7]

'Philosopher Sir Karl Popper said, "If we are uncritical, we shall always find what we want: we shall look for, and find, confirmations and we shall look away from, and not see, whatever might be dangerous to our pet theories. In this way, it is only too easy to obtain what appears to be overwhelming evidence in favour of a theory which, if approached critically, would have been refuted.' [8]

And Sir David Attenborough in a widely reported statement on 23 January 2019: 'We can create a world with clean air and water, unlimited energy and fish stocks that will sustain us well into the future. But to do that, we need a plan.'

ooOoo

I have four children, six grandchildren, and three great grandchildren. They will have to inhabit the environment I and my contemporaries bequeath to them. When I read reports like those citing damning evidence of environmental vandalism against Adani, the company seeking to open the Carmichael coal mine in Queensland, I'm really worried...

The Scriptures

Last year – 2019 – in our church, we concentrated on creation/nature for six weeks. We heard statements like these from our worship-leader and preacher:

(1) Psalm 19 suggests we find God in two important 'books' - Nature and Scripture. Paul borrows that idea in Romans 1: 'For since the creation of the world God's invisible qualities - his eternal power and divine nature - have been clearly seen, being understood from what has been made, so that people are without excuse.' And then there's Martin Luther: 'God writes the Gospel, not in the Bible alone, but also on trees, in the flowers, and clouds and stars'.

(2) Many churches celebrate Earth Day, St Francis of Assisi Day, on the first Sunday in October. In 2007, an ecumenical

conference in Romania recommended that on this day we be 'dedicated to prayer for the protection of Creation and the promotion of sustainable lifestyles that reverse our contribution to climate change'. [9a]

And from one of Rev. Jim Barr's sermons, this apt quote: 'There is one question we must address, the most important question that has ever been asked in human history, a question that should be uppermost in everyone's mind, a question that's been hanging over everyone's head for many years, becoming more urgent every year, and the question is whether organised human life will indeed survive. This is not a question about the distant future. It must be answered in this generation.' (Noam Chomsky - 2018). [9b]

The Facts [10]

'Scientific evidence for warming of the climate system is unequivocal.' (Intergovernmental Panel on Climate Change) [11]

Australia has about 1.3% of global greenhouse emissions, but we make up just 0.3% of the world's population and have one of the highest per person emissions rates in the world. 'In 2017 Australia pumped 533.7 million tonnes of greenhouse gases into the atmosphere - a seven-year high... Electricity generation is the single biggest contributor, at 33.7%. The sector is still heavily reliant on coal, despite the move towards renewable energy... The opposition Labor Party's emissions reduction goal is relatively ambitious - 45% by 2030, based on 2005 levels - but 'critics say it is still inconsistent with keeping global warming to 1.5 degrees and fails to address the coal problem... The Greens wants a ban on coal mining, burning or exporting by 2030.' [12]

'The Intergovernmental Panel on Climate Change: About one million animal and plant species are threatened with extinction, many within decades, more than ever in human history... The main culprits are, in ascending order: changes in land and sea use, direct exploitation of organisms; climate change; pollution and invasive alien species. Three-quarters of the land-based environment and about 66% of the marine environment have been significantly altered by human actions. More than one-third of the world's land surface and nearly 75% of freshwater resources are now devoted to crop or livestock production.' [13]

'Australia's record on land clearing is poor'; let us do more to protect the forests and other ecosystems we have now and build out from there... And 'as a society we need to fundamentally rethink our economic goals. We can't afford endless growth.' [But] there are signs of hope. Britain recently experienced more than a week without using coal to generate electricity for the first time since Queen Victoria was on the throne, and the country is on track to have a carbon-neutral electricity system by 2025... Meanwhile New Zealand has just introduced a price on carbon with multi-partisan support.' [14]

'Climate policy has been littered with broken promises ever since the 1992 Earth Summit in Rio de Janeiro. Indeed the core promises written into the Paris agreement (2015) are not being met. A recent study reveals that only 17 countries - the likes of

Samoa and Algeria - are living up to their promises to reduce carbon-emission growth, and only because they promised to do very, very little... Australia's promise in 2015... committed the country to a pathway towards finding cheaper and better alternatives to fossil fuels. More than three years have passed with little to show for it.' [15]

'China and India, No 1 and No 3 respectively of the top global emitters, have not committed to start to reduce carbon intensity, let alone total co2 output, until 2030. (The US. has had some success in reducing emissions, though still short of the Paris commitments it is withdrawing from. It has achieved this on the back of fracking for natural gas.)' [16]

'The 2019 report for the Intergovernmental Science-Policy Platform on Biodiversity and Ecosystems Services revealed the pace of destruction was as much as 100 times faster than the natural rate over the past 10 million years... According to the last report of the UN's Intergovernmental Panel on Climate Change in October 2018, we have only 12 years to halve emissions - and almost eliminate them by 2050 - to keep the rise in temperature around 2 degrees above pre-industrial levels. Exceeding 2 degrees could trigger irreversible tipping points.' [17]

'As perhaps the highest per capita polluter on the planet, and the second largest exporter of coal and LNG, our international responsibilities are clear... Consider the monumental cost of inaction: extreme weather, financial collapses, the unprecedented loss of biodiversity, species extinction, and, ultimately, destruction of the planet itself... During the recent student climate protests, students from a Byron Bay school stood in public and traced out the anthem "Our Future".' [18]

Ian Dunlop is a former international oil, gas and coal industry executive. In a newspaper article (14 March 2019), he wrote that current fossil fuel projects (including Adani, and 20 NSW coal projects) are 'crimes against humanity. Fossil fuel investment must stop, now. Dangerous climate change is occurring with the 1 degree warming already experienced. The lower 1.5 degree limit of the Paris Agreement will be here this decade... On our current emissions trajectory, warming will be 3-4 degrees long before 2100... The current climate and energy debate is irrelevant. Our emissions must be cut by 50% by 2030, and 100% by 2050.' [19]

'A 2019 report from the CSIRO says the lowest-cost power from a *newly built* facility is now produced by solar and wind... Professor Ross Garnaut from the University of Melbourne has said "nowhere in the developed world are solar and wind resources together so abundant as in the west-facing coasts and peninsulas of southern Australia. Play our cards right, and Australia's exceptionally rich endowment per person in renewable energy resources makes us a low-cost location for energy supply in a low-carbon world economy."' [20]

Just today, as I write, Phillip Adams has an article about his friend (the intellectual and former Federal politician) Barry Jones who 40 years ago created a Commission for the Future, hopefully building bridges between scientists, the public, and politicians. Phillip was asked to chair it, and at one of the first meetings he posed the 'T. S. Eliot Question' to a panel of top

Nobel prize-winning scientists: 'How will the world end – with a bang or a whimper?' Responses? Nuclear war, interfering with nature in terms of genetic modification, artificial intelligence and robotics pushing humans aside, etc....

'Finally a quiet voice silenced everybody. Most had never heard of the "greenhouse effect", understood since the 19th century, and this scientist and his colleagues around the world were seeing it happen every day on the dials in our laboratories - the inexorable increase in "greenhouse gases" caused by burning fossil fuels. He told us that if something wasn't done, and soon, the planet would become for creatures like ourselves, uninhabitable...'

What happened to that commission? 'After Barry Jones' era, some governments didn't bother having ministers for science... the Commission of the Future ran out of future... First defunded, then privatised, it then disappeared.' [21]

Why? 'Money, money, money' of course. I saw a program on the ABC yesterday about how much lobbyists are paid by corporations to change the minds of our elected representatives, politicians...

When you ask Google to provide Climate Change facts, you find this on the first page (from the Environmental Defense Fund, my summary): '7 facts about climate change that are 100% true, no matter what Trump says:

1. Climate change is real and man-made, and there is overwhelming scientific consensus (97% of climate scientists worldwide) that this is true.

2. All major climate change reports are thoroughly researched and based on the most accurate, up-to-date science.

3. Climate change reports from major climate science institutions around the world are entirely based on thoroughly peer-reviewed scientific research.

4. Working to stop climate change can drive economic growth, while unchecked climate change is expected to have dire economic consequences. For example, Citibank estimates the costs of unchecked climate change at more than $40 trillion by 2060.

5. Climate scientists are underpaid — or not paid at all — for their work. They earn less than most other academics.

6. Federal climate change reports are credible because they are written by scientists, not politicians.

7. 'Major climate change assessments from reputable scientific institutions — such as the U.S. government's National Climate Assessment and the UN's Intergovernmental Panel on Climate Change's special report on different levels of warming — consider a wide range of future conditions, from the use of advanced technologies that remove carbon dioxide from the atmosphere, to escalating emissions from the absence of climate action.' [22]

Another important item on Google's first page: David Attenborough's current documentary which looks at a planet on the verge of climate catastrophe, with its intimate stories of people's lives affected by climate change. [23]

Then there's the Climate Council: 'constantly refuting misinformation and climate myths in the media...

'The Federal and Queensland governments should be ashamed of themselves for contemplating using $1billion of taxpayers' money to shore up the fossil-fuel industry and thereby risking the health of our children.

'Local communities will fare badly. The Carmichael mine will destroy the environment around the Galilee Basin for it is inconceivable that it will not adversely affect groundwater that will then seep into the alluvial basin. It's very likely it will also adversely impact the Great Barrier Reef. All Australians who care about the health of this country and its inhabitants should read the Adani files and say to their politicians "No to using our money for your political agendas".'

An important item on their website: Climate Policies of the Major Australian Political Parties:
Liberal-National Party Climate Solutions Package
Australian Labor Party Labor's Climate Change Action Plan
Australian Greens announce climate and energy plan [24].

'Global warming is going to exact a brutal toll not only on natural landscapes and agriculture but on wildlife, with countless thousands of species set to be extinguished before our very eyes... But there is one creature whose disappearance by 2040 is all but guaranteed: the climate sceptic. "In 30 years' time, the effects of climate change will be so obvious that no one will be able to deny it".' [25]

More jottings on climate change

* Teen climate activist Swede Greta Thunberg sailed from Plymouth, England to New York Harbour, in her carbon emission-free sailboat. Her message to reporters: 'Just listen to the science'. She said that having Aspergers means she does not 'fall for lies'. [26]

* National President of the ALP, Wayne Swan: 'Australia produces about 4% of the world's thermal coal. If we're going to reduce emissions in Australia, 19% of our emissions come out of the transport sector...' To which the founder of Doctors for the Environment, David Shearman, responded: 'Current water extraction for 6000 coal seam gas wells (in Queensland) is about 60,000 megalitres a year... All other use of precious water by industry, agriculture and humans in this region? 164,000 ML a year' [27]

* David Attenborough: 'We are now so numerous, so powerful, so all-pervasive... that we can actually exterminate whole ecosystems without even noticing it...' He went on to hail the 2015 Paris climate agreement as a point where world leaders had recognised the dangers of rising temperatures, but 'this has not been universal... There have been people who have withdrawn from that.' [28]

* 'Despite the climate crisis, there is no shortage of fresh water', writes Phillip Adams in an article on Max

Whisson, climate scientist. He continues: 'According to a US Geological Survey, at any one time the atmosphere contains around 12,900 cubic kilometres of water - enough to cover the entire surface of the planet, land and oceans, with an inch of rain.' Adams continues: 'He - Whisson - invented simple ways to access it... His "Whisson Windmill" was elegant and simple: it's a vertical windmill that could power a condenser that would produce water anywhere you put it. Place them in the Nullabor (desert) and you'd create little oases...' Funding? None. 'A tragedy. Max didn't want money for himself - he wanted to donate his ideas.' In May 2019 he passed away... [29]

* 'Carrying more than 4 billion passengers last year, the global aviation industry is responsible for about 2.5% of the world's carbon emissions - a bigger contribution than Australia's'... IATA - whose 290 members account for 82% of the world's air traffic - has pledged that by 2050 it will have cut its carbon output to half what it was in 2005.' [30]

And on the twin topic: caring for creation

A Christian response to all this? From Genesis onwards, humans are instructed to care for creation. A Conference of Catholic bishops gave us a good summary:

Genesis 1:1-31 God made the heavens and the earth and it was good.

Genesis 2:15 Humans are commanded to care for God's creation.

Leviticus 25:1-7 The land itself must be given a rest and not abused.

Deuteronomy 10:14 All of heaven and earth belong to the Lord.

Psalm 24:1-2 All the earth is the Lord's.

Daniel 3:56-82 Creation proclaims the glory of God.

Matthew 6:25-34 God loves and cares for all of creation.

Romans 1:20 Creation reveals the nature of God.

1 Corinthians 10:26 The earth and its fullness are the Lord's.

[31]

ooOoo

So where do we start? Here's a potpourri of suggestions:

\# Don't throw plastic bottle-tops into the garbage: some sea-creatures have been found to have lots of them in their stomachs. In our home we collect them to be melted down; one church collected plastic caps of various kinds which were sent to a company to make a bench for daycare play area.

\# Australia has 6 million feral cats: they are the single biggest threat to our native animals, and have already driven to extinction 20 of the 30 mammals lost. Cull the cats? We have no choice. It's a race to save 124 species of wild life, and feral cats are notoriously hard to kill.

\# Cooling in the stratospheres is causing it to shrink, lowering that layer by "a number of kilometres" NASA noted recently... Rising temperatures - with an

El Nino boost - drove 2014, 2015 and 2016 to record-breaking warmth.

\# A recent report by the Green Institute found that about $1billion Emissions Reduction Fund money spent so far has gone into conserving mulga-dominated areas of south-west Queensland and western NSW on land that might not have been cleared anyway. [32]

\# 'The war on renewable energy is entering its final, desperate stages. It is inevitable that Australia and the world will soon be entirely powered by the wind, sun, waves and water. The only questions left are whether that will happen in time to prevent the worst impacts of global warming, if coal-mining communities will be supported through the transition, and exactly when the Coalition will crawl out of its ideological bunker and realise the battle is already over. What makes me so sure that the game is up for fossil fuels? It's not the increasing shrillness of a national Treasurer fondling a lump of coal in our parliament, or the "truth overboard" attempts to blame renewable energy for everything from South Australian blackouts to arrested production at Alcoa's Portland aluminium smelter.

'In the US, coal-burning power stations are dropping like dominoes – 94 closed their doors in 2015 and another 41 closed in 2016. In this financial landscape, ageing coal generators are like the last mature specimens of a once dominant species, unable to reproduce and therefore ultimately doomed to extinction.

'Coal is going the way of the fax machine and typewriter – once useful, now superseded. If politicians keep fighting yesterday's battles, they'll make themselves redundant too. Mark Wakeham is CEO of Environment Victoria. [33]

Endnotes

[1] *Note 1*: An excellent contra but generally irenic article by a NZ University of Canterbury lecturer in geology named David Shelley concludes: 'The very idea that we can stop climate change is barking mad. Climate change is inevitable, as geology has always shown.' Google it or see his article in *The Australian*, 8 July 2019, p. 12.

Note 2: The Australian PM's line that 'Australia alone cannot cool the planet' is, according to *The Age* editorial 17 August 2019, p. 34, 'a classic excuse to do nothing.' (And an approach which resulted in one South Pacific head of state being reduced to tears!)

Note 3: On the other hand, young people are skipping school all over the (Western) world to publicly protest against climate denialism. 'The young people have science and history on their side', asserts an *Age* newspaper editorial. 'Only fringe ideologues continue to reject the reality of existentially dangerous anthropogenic global warming... Young people focus on the future and they vote, or soon

will be able to. They are informed, articulate and committed.' *The Age*, 1 December 2018.
- [2] *Sydney Morning Herald*, 20 December 2018.
- [3] *The Australian*, 23 October 2018, p. 23.
- [4] *The Australian*, 8 February 2019, p. 3.
- [5] *The Australian*, 6 February 2019, p. 11.
- [6] *The Age*, 1 February 2019, p. 18.
- [7] *The Age, Good Weekend*, 26 January 2019.
- [8] Letters to Editor, *The Australian*, 23 January 2019, p. 11.
- [9a] Mary Edgar, Box Hill Baptist Church, 1 September 2019
- [9b] Rev. Jim Barr, ibid.
- [10] Visit here for an excellent summary of the effects of global warming on humans: https://en.wikipedia.org/wiki/Effects_of_global_warming_on_humans
- [11] Ben Weir, 'The warming seas cooking our ecosystems,' The Age, 20/12/2018, p. 11.
- [12] 'Tracking your vote on climate Explainer.' *The Age*, 13 May 2019, p. 12.
- [13] Graham Lloyd, 'Evolution of Climate Fear', *The Australian*, 21 May 2019, p. 11.
- [14] Caitlin Fitzsimmons, 'Focus Now on a Planet in Danger', *The Sunday Age*, 12 May 2019, p. 37.
- [15] Bjorn Lomborg, 'Research Funds are central to a climate solution', *Herald-Sun*, 13 May 2019, p. 23.
- [16] *The Australian*, 13 May, p. 24.
- [17] *The Sunday Age* editorial, 12 May 2019, p. 34.

[18] John Hewson, former Liberal opposition leader, *The Age*, 9 May 2019, p. 21.
[19] *The Age*, 14 March 2019, p. 22.
[20] Ross Gittins, *The Age*, 13 February 2019, p. 20.
[21] Barry Jones, *The Weekend Australian Magazine*, 31 August 2019, p. 66.
[22] Environmental Defense Fund, https://www.edf.org/climate/how-climate-change-plunders-planet/climate-facts
[23] https://iview.abc.net.au/show/climate-change-the-facts
[24] https://www.climatecouncil.org.au/resources/factsheet-climate-policies-major-australian-political-parties/
[25] Prof. Lesley Hughes, of the biological sciences department at Sydney's Macquarie University. Reported in *The Age, Good Weekend 30th Anniversary Issue*, 27 September 2014, p. 35.
[26] Reuters, *The Times*, 29 August 2019.
[27] *The Age*, 30 August 2019, p. 21.
[28] *The Australian*, 24 January 2019, p. 8.
[29] Phillip Adams, 'Farewell, my inventive friend', *The Weekend Australian*, 8-9 June 2019, p. 58.
[30] Patrick Hatch, 'Climate Change a threat to airlines', *The Age*, 8 June 2019, p. 10.
[31] http://www.usccb.org/beliefs-and-teachings/what-we-believe/catholic-social-teaching/care-for-creation.cfm

[32] Peter Hannon, *The Sunday Age*, 6 November 2016 p. 7.

[33] http://www.smh.com.au/comment/reality-check-malcolm-youve-already-lost-the-war-on-renewables-20170309-guu4fq.html

Chapter 5
KEN R. MANLEY

The writer of Genesis (39:3, Tyndale's translation) tells us that 'the Lord was with Joseph, and he was a luckie fellowe'. A Victorian Baptist pastor/leader, Rev. Tom Keyte, borrowed that phrase for the title of his autobiography (published in the 1960s): *The Chronicles of a "Luckie Fellowe"*.

I thought of that as I read another Baptist leader, Ken Manley's 2018 'whole of life' story. It was also aptly titled: *For All That Has Been - Thanks!*. I've now read it twice: Ken was certainly a lucky fellow. So are we who count him as a friend.

His 84 years of living, serving as a historian/scholar-pastor-teacher, have been as rich and multi-faceted as anyone's I know.

Just one variable: there must be about 100 people in his story whom he describes as being a 'special friend' or just 'friend'. Lucky fellow!

Working backwards, Ken was part of an interesting migration of Baptist pastors from NSW to Victoria. At one stage back in the 1970s, someone counted 32 of us - with just two Victorian/Whitley graduates moving to ministry north of the Murray. When the NSW Baptist leadership wondered about all that, they sent two of their number to Victoria to wander around, attend some of our churches (the two largest had NSW-trained senior pastors) and talk to many of the pastors who were part of that migration. [1] Their report, in brief: 'Victorian Baptists are more open to progressive ideas, like, for example, concerning the ordination of women...' (PS. No one among

NSW Baptist Union leaders I've asked has sighted that report! It was never shared with the denomination-at-large). [2]

Ken joined that migration a decade later - 1987, as Principal of Whitley (Baptist) College in Melbourne, and - as you read this autobiography carefully - perhaps partly for the same reasons. [3]

Tim Costello's Foreword (he launched the book in June 2018) summarises it all very well in this paragraph:

> In this book, a broad yet detailed portrayal of his years, one cannot help but be impressed by the interplay of all the following: early family influences and humble origins in Sydney; student days taking him to strutting the halls of Bristol and Oxford Universities; a first-class mind delving into the rich veins of history; pastoral work that captures his empathy, preparation of sermons and casting of vision for congregations he served; his diligent work exploring the significance and nuances of the story of being Baptist - both local and worldwide; the deft handling of complex theological issues and debates; his years of leading Whitley, a great Australian theological college; ecumenical tussles entered into and carefully chronicled; and all this while enjoying the splendid travel experiences he takes us on, and meeting a 'who's who' of global personalities and leaders that he knows and regards as his friends. Ken, you have had not just a "fortunate life" but also a magnificent one. [4]

Ken says he has three motivations for writing this memoir: (1) So that his children and grandchildren will understand more about their heritage; (2) Others might be interested in 'how a fair-haired youngster running around in bare feet ended up becoming a Baptist minister and graduating with a doctoral degree from the University of Oxford'; and (3) 'I have been singularly blessed... and I would like to invite others to know why I feel this way.' Touché!

And the title? From the well-known prayer of Dag Hammarskjold: 'For all that has been - Thanks! To all that shall be - Yes!'

Some aspects of his childhood journey I found interesting: He writes: 'I have often been placed in the situation of an outsider': *At the age of nine he became the only Protestant in a large Catholic school. And at that tender age he had to travel several train stations to get there. *At the age of 16 he graduated from an 'unremarkable' primary and secondary education to Balmain Teachers' College where he 'came alive academically'. * From a nominal Anglican background he found a sincere faith in a Baptist Church. * And finally he moved from a Sydney pastorate (NSW Baptists' largest church) to be Principal of Whitley College in Melbourne.

Ken was born into a 'family with secrets' (I won't spoil it for you!) in 1935, and lived his childhood years in a humble Sydney suburban area (Bankstown/Yagoona). I inhabited four homes a few miles east: first at Mortdale then Oatley, and like Ken enjoyed swimming in the Georges River (Ken was slightly more upstream!).

One episode you won't often read about in a book like this: he was sexually abused by a church leader at about the age of 10 or 11. Fortunately, Ken says the experience did not deeply scar him...

And theologically, his experience in a Catholic school meant he could never embrace 'the militant anti-Catholicism that many Protestants, not least Baptists, have often demonstrated...' The principal, Brother Xavier was especially warm towards him, and when he left the school gave him a gift of Thomas a Kempis' classic *The Imitation of Christ*, a book Ken has treasured ever since. That provides another clue, I think, to his irenic progressive theological stance. Fortunately his experience as a teenager at Yagoona Baptist Church with a couple of eminently gifted pastors also provided a sound theological foundation. [5] As a late teenager, he was given many opportunities to preach here and there in Baptist churches.

A pervasive theme is also Ken's love of sport: I lost count of the number of varied sporting teams where he was asked to captain. Mind you, they weren't all successful: once his high school's Second XIII rugby league team was defeated by something in the order of 100 to nil!

After passing his Leaving Certificate, he received a scholarship covering his two-year education at Balmain Teachers' College (1952-53). His lecturers there were excellent teachers. He received good academic grades, and of course also participated in the College's Rugby Union and cricket teams... But he also became President of the College's Evangelical Union.

He did the required stint of the Australian Government's National Service after he graduated, which provided some rich experiences, and also helped him to become physically fit. Then, four years of teaching here and there. He must have caught the eye of the educational authorities, as he was offered a position at Wagga Wagga Demonstration School. He became president of the Wagga Teachers' Christian Fellowship and in the Baptist Church there he met a man renowned among NSW Baptists for his reputation as a powerful conservative and for being an 'awkward' - but 'extremely capable' - deacon.

Ken then spent four years (1958-61) at the Ashfield campus of the seminary which trained pastors for the Baptist ministry in NSW (it later became known as Morling College). It was also a very rich experience. For three reasons: 'Here I began serious theological study, here I made some of my closest lifelong friends, and whilst there I began to serve as the pastor of a local church'.

'Academically', writes Ken, 'I managed to pass every subject with generally encouraging results' (in spite of there being 'some irrelevant and poorly taught subjects'. The principal was 'Prof. Morling' (as he was affectionately known); vice-principal Gilbert Wright (main contribution - a pastoral one as students remember him); then Rev. John Thompson ('with a string of degrees' - 'an outstanding lecturer'). The curriculum majored on Bible ('missing were subjects such as Ethics, Missiology, Philosophy and Apologetics'). An interesting sentence: 'A former missionary, Rev. Neville Andersen... taught us Old Testament in our last year as John

Thompson was on study leave at Cambridge. He was able to use John Thompson's notes but inevitably his classes lacked the brilliance of John.'

Narwee Baptist Church (1959-61)

As I began studying for the Baptist ministry (1964-7) a couple of years after Ken left the College (for Bristol), we had not had much contact. But what we had in common were 'student ministries' at Narwee Baptist Church ('NBC' as we affectionately called that wonderful congregation). [7] This is Ken's story, not mine, but in his three years as a single student pastor, and later my four years as their first married student pastor, the church grew significantly.

That – for both of us – is a special story on its own. Ken writes: 'My appointment to Narwee proved to be a great blessing to me and a strong confirmation of my call to pastoral ministry'. (I would endorse that for Jan and myself too). Among the many highlights of Ken's time at Narwee was the church's participation in the Billy Graham Crusade. [8]

Ken married Margaret at Campsie Baptist Church on 6 January 1962. He quotes Winston Churchill: 'My most brilliant achievement was my ability to persuade my wife to marry me'. Ken: 'I also regard Margaret's acceptance of my proposal as the most significant event in my adult life'.

An important sequel: Ken's love for his wife, and his gratitude for the sacrifices she made for him to complete his academic work in England (and since) is one of the most touching elements of his story. During the five years Ken was persuading scholars in Bristol and Oxford to accept his academic writings, Margaret 'plied her trade' as a pharmacist. Ken's lavish praise for her sacrifices - including the postponement of their return to Australia, and having children there (two gorgeous girls) - is a tribute to both of them, and makes reading about this marriage narrative covering fifty-something years a tonic! It's worth buying the book to be touched by all that on its own: don't just take my word for it!

And a few other notes

You can read more in the rest of the book about Ken's adventures in scholarship and writing - including details of the subject of his Oxford doctorate - John Rippon (1751-1836) - and many other aspects of Baptist faith and life - throughout the world, and back into history; his pastorates (Narwee; Faringdon in England; Armidale, Pymble, and Epping in NSW; his theological teaching in Adelaide, Sydney, and Melbourne (as Principal of Whitley College from 1987 to 2000); his occasional forays into Baptist debates and positions of honour, especially in the Baptist Unions of South Australia, NSW, and finally in Victoria... Then there were wonderful family holidays and travel adventures...

Ken is more gracious than I am when critiquing the heresies/ stupidities (my words) of various Baptist entities: *Examples* (his words): 'Developments among some Southern Baptists are disconcerting'; 'some uncomfortable and irritating developments in the [NSW Baptist] Denomination' included 'poor handling' of some fundamentalist-vs.-mainline

Evangelical concepts to do with a literal six-day creation etc.; and the College's possibly being in cahoots with some Roman Catholics, etc.

Time would fail Ken – and me – to recount the efforts of Baptist folks (often in rural churches) who'd like their denomination to mandate certain doctrinaire positions on matters such as the inerrancy of the Bible, accepting LGBTI people in positions of leadership, and the ordination of women into positions of pastoral/academic etc. leadership...

There are so many Manley peregrinations – with their opportunities for Ken to give addresses in many places – described in the second half of this book. Buy it and be challenged! We can't do justice to them all. Here's an excerpt from just one address he gave as President of the Baptist Union of Victoria: 'God is always calling us to be more than we have been. The future church may not be the one we expect or even want... No-one can predict the Lord's "surprise moves". A new church is right now being born around us, a church with deep roots in the past and shaped by present needs - for future church exists not for our comfort but to serve the world still loved so passionately by our God.' [9]

Ken's practice of 'never [having] an unpublished thought' – a phrase often used to describe the Catholic priest, Andrew Greeley, who had published about 50 best-selling novels and more than 100 nonfiction stories in his lifetime - is nowhere better expressed than in his chapter on his articles in *The Australian Baptist* magazine (4 September 974 until December 1991: 362 columns, total 200,000 words – 'the word equivalent of two doctoral theses'). It's now more than a quarter of a century since he wrote his last column, but the issues he opened up are still debated in/between Baptist groups: various competing theories about the second coming and the inspiration of the Bible, the ordination of women, open vs. closed membership, 'evangelicals' vs. 'fundamentalists' etc. etc. Feedback helped Ken discern that Baptists in Tasmania, NSW and Queensland were the most conservative; Victorians and South Australians are most progressive. [10]

Morris West, formerly Principal of Bristol College, joked about retirement, 'I think it's a job for a younger man.' Ken wrote: 'Like so many before me, I have often wondered how I managed to fit in time for work'. Ken traveled widely to Baptist World Alliance meetings - he was a vice-president at one stage - speaking engagements, writing (including chapters in three of my *Still Waters Deep Waters* series of devotional books), holidays, etc. Their two daughters Lynda and Susan married men who were ministers (Baptist and Anglican respectively), producing three daughters and two sons (again, respectively): very happy families, and a joy to these doting grandparents. This amazing book can be purchased securely online at *www.underthesun.net.au.*

Endnotes

[1] Jack Simmonds at Blackburn North, and myself at Blackburn.

[2] Prof. Keith Dyer – New Testament, Whitley College – had written a progressive view of LGBTI issues in a paper about 20+ years ago.

[3] The Baptists in the U.S. have a more highly contrasting critique of each other: The Southern Baptist Convention recently mandated 'no women in leadership.' The more progressive American Baptist Churches denomination are mostly flexible on this and other issues. Another way to test the flavour of each ideological stance: the drift of gifted progressive Southern Baptists – like Dr John Claypool – away from that denomination, or to its margins... (There's a chapter on John Claypool in *Questions and Responses, Volume 2*.)

[4] Bert Facey, *A Fortunate Life* (1981), referred to on p.10. Tim Costello is a well-known Australian Baptist pastor - and stirrer on socio-political issues. See chapter 2 of this book.

[5] p. 60. David Stewart, later to become principal of the NZ Bible Institute (who, incidentally, once offered me a teaching post there), and Noel Vose, founding principal of the WA Baptist Seminary, and who became the only Australian Baptist to be appointed President of the Baptist World Alliance. (I got to know Noel as I visited that College a few times when he was Principal; and he was on the Board of World Vision when I was employed by them to be an Australian 'Minister at Large' for a decade.)

[6] The new Principal E. Roberts-Thompson came during Ken's final year, and was soon driven out of the College by the NSW Baptist authorities - 'too liberal' - to join the Presbyterians (then not so

conservative). In my first three years - I commuted 40 minutes each way by car for four years from Narwee to Morling College two years after Ken left - I managed to avoid Neville Anderson's classes on Church History but he made a special point of 'inviting' me during my fourth year: frankly, it was a waste of time (note the stronger critique than the more nuanced one Ken made). But Neville and I became friends after he moved to Melbourne to be Principal of the 'Melbourne Bible Institute' where he invited me to teach a few courses and speak to the student assemblies from time to time. (More often than I was invited to Whitley College, for some reason!) In his retirement, he was an interim pastor of a Baptist Church in a southern Sydney suburb, which became something of a mess: he once wrote to me asking for advice on that situation. Ken was editor of *Summa Supremo*, the College's once-a-year journal, in his last year as I was later in my final year.

[7] When Jan and I left NBC the membership was approaching 100, and the church had three stipended staff - and a lot of young people. They invited Rev. Mike Dennis to come from W.A. to take over - and the church continued to grow. For details of NBC's history see J. Maitland, *Together in Christ*. Narwee Baptist Church 1954-2004.

[8] 'In total, almost 3.25 million attended the Graham meetings in Australia and New Zealand with some

130,000 Australians indicating that they had made a spiritual decision to accept Christ at the meetings.' p. 110.

[9] K.R. Manley (ed.), *Future Church: a Baptist Discussion*, Hawthorn: Baptist Union of Victoria, 1996, pp. 27-28.

[10] He once referred to an essay by Martin Marty who argued that 'evangelicals' were the true heirs of people like Wesley, Whitfield, and Wilberforce; but fundamentalists had schismatic and militant tendencies - fragmentation, separationism and censoriousness. These two groups had differing approaches as well to 'social sins' (movies, theatre, dancing, smoking, liquor): evangelicals tended to allow more freedom and were opposed to hard legalisms about such issues.

Chapter 6
LGBTIS ARE LOVED BY GOD TOO!

* 'Our son is gay. We attended an Evangelical church that preached love for all people – gay or straight. But our son only experienced rejection. The elders told him "You may be homosexual but you cannot live according to your true identity". He didn't get invited to friends' family parties etc. Perhaps they feared his homosexuality was contagious? It's been a lonely journey for our family. The only healing, unfortunately, has come from outside the church. But we miss the koinonia we experienced there. What should we do?'

* Champion swimmer Ian Thorpe says he "concealed his sexuality out of fear". Ian is one of the three highest-profile gay men in Australia – with Federal Greens politician Dr Bob Brown and retired High Court judge, Justice Michael Kirby.

ooOoo

'For every complex problem there is an answer that is clear, simple and wrong.' (H. L. Mencken)

'One can resist the invasion of armies; one cannot resist the invasion of ideas.' (Victor Hugo)

'Nothing is more sad than the death of an illusion.' (Arthur Koestler).

John Maynard Keynes: 'When the "facts" change, I change my mind. And you, sir?'

Imagine a bell curve... Radicals are on the left; next to them are Progressives; to the right of them are Conservatives; and on the far right are Traditionalists.

Radicals are driven, mostly, by anger at injustices served up by dominant authority-figures and structures to marginalised people and groups.

Traditionalists have fear as their dominant emotion. They're afraid of change and the cognitive dissonance that causes.

Disclosure: I – Rowland Croucher – have moved from a Conservative to a Progressive stance on most of this. (I was media spokesperson for the Victorian Festival of Light in the 1970s.) I did this by listening to LGBTI folks' stories (dominant themes: pain and rejection), studying the science (all relevant major Western scientific bodies assert 'they were born that way'), exploring Biblical hermeneutics again on the topic, and even identifying with LGBTI's by marching in the 2014 Sydney Mardi Gras.

A little further – important – note. I am critical of Radicals to my left, who won't allow people to change their opinions at their own pace. And I'm critical of the Traditionalists whose motto on all this seems to be 'Don't confuse me with facts, my mind's made up'.

And I'm critical of myself when I don't live up to this admonition by St Paul: 'Live creatively, friends. If someone falls into sin, forgivingly restore them, saving your critical comments for yourself. You might be needing forgiveness before the day's out. Stoop down and reach out to those who are oppressed. Share their burdens, and so complete Christ's law. If you think you are too good for that, you are badly deceived.' Galatians 6:2 (*The Message* version).

ooOoo

I was invited, a few years ago now, by a group of Christian LGBTI communities to be their Australia-wide chaplain. So far, we have just one chapter in these *Questions & Responses* books about LGBTI issues: 'Marriage Equality' in Book 2. For Q&R4, the next volume (*Deo volente*, parousia permitting! etc.), I hope to have written on the ruckus surrounding Australian rugby player Israel Folau's warning that 'homosexuals' are going to hell, and the debate going on in our Australian parliament about legislation unpinning personal and corporate freedoms. (Can't wait to read what I write on all that!).

So what are the headlines?

A while back, I registered a Google Alert request: send me articles as they are published using these words in the search: 'Homosexuality' 'changed' 'mind'. I now have over a hundred of them. Here in one chapter (!) we'll summarise the key issues, from that list and other sources. You can follow up with some relevant Googling.

STOP PRESS: As I write, Australia has a new Prime Minister, Scott Morrison (a staunch Pentecostal) whose right-wing Liberal Party had written a letter to the LGBTI community scrambling for votes, giving assurances about legislating against gay 'conversion therapy' which went beyond the PM's stance: he'd spent months saying the matter was 'not an issue' for him. His party's letter also promised changes to the *Family Law Act* that could make the system more inclusive for LGBTI couples and children.

Now we have press articles where the commentariat are saying the Labor Party surprisingly lost that election because it was seen to be too pro-gay. Here's a typical headline: 'Religious seats punish ALP for loss of freedom'. All but two of the nation's ten most religious seats (where protesters waved placards reading 'Hands off our religious freedom' and 'Hands off our mosques'), chiefly Labor strongholds in western Sydney, recorded swings to the Coalition at the 2019 election.

And what's the 'religious freedom' the Coalition parties, now in Government - and Pentecostal or other Conservative Churches including some with predominantly South Pacific congregations - want? As one LGBTI spokesperson (who prefers to remain anonymous) put it: 'Simple: fundamentalist Christians and Muslims want the freedom to discriminate against gay people! And this includes conservative Sydney Anglican churches, 34 of whom on 25 October 2018 wrote to Federal MPs urging them to protect exemptions that currently permit them to fire or expel LGBTIQ staff and students. [1] And the freedom to castigate congregations, for example in the more inclusive Uniting Church, which are more accepting/ welcoming of LGBTI worshippers.'

1. WHAT DO THE SCIENTISTS (and Legislators) SAY?

(Check any of these on Google Search). 1905: 'Homosexuals are not sick people', and 1930: 'Punishing homosexuality is an extreme violation of human rights' (Sigmund Freud); 1935: Aversion therapy (electric shocks to testicles): Louis Max (New York) reports no long term cures; 1948: Kinsey: 4% white males exclusively homosexual throughout their lives, post adolescence. 2-6% females exclusively homosexual; 1967: UK decriminalises private homosexual acts between consenting adults; 1973 American Psychiatric Association: 'no longer an illness'; 1975: South Australia repeals sodomy law; other states/territories 1976-1990, (Tasmania 1997); 1991: Larger numbers of homosexual youth attempt or commit suicide (G. Remafedi); homosexual men with identical twin brothers much more likely to be homosexual than if they had fraternal twin brother (Bailey & Pillard); 2001: Report on reparative therapies' lack of success (Shidlo & Schroeder); but Robert Spitzer: some highly motivated individuals can change from gay to straight. (Spitzer recants in 2012); 2003: US Supreme Court decriminalises private consensual adult homosexual behaviour; 2004: Gene Robinson - first openly gay person to become a bishop in Episcopal traditions; 2013: An Australian Report which interviewed 1000 LGBTIs found that 42 per cent thought about self-harm or suicide - making them six times more likely to consider taking their own lives than heterosexual peers; 2018: 425,000 Australians are thought to be intersex - about the same number of people with red hair [2]; 2019: Same-sex marriage is now legally performed and recognised (nationwide or in some jurisdictions) in 28 countries; 2019: Both political leaders in the Australian election fled from the issue of commenting on Israel Folau's diatribe against 'homosexuals', despite its obvious importance to ordinary people; Recent (2019) NBC-Wall Street Journal poll: 'Nearly 70% of Americans said they'd be either enthusiastic or comfortable with a Presidential candidate who is gay or lesbian'.

2. WHAT DOES THE BIBLE SAY?

An interview on Google with a well-known Bible Translator is titled 'Eugene Peterson on changing his mind about same-sex issues and marriage'. Excerpt: 'Peterson's popular paraphrase of the Bible – *The Message* – doesn't use the words 'homosexual' or 'homosexuality' – 'which is not proof of anything. After all, those words never appear in any English translation of the Bible until 1946.'

UK church leader Steven Chalke says 'juvenile' interpretations of the Bible endanger gay people. [3] He asserts that the Bible has been used throughout history to oppress LGBT communities. 'And still the Bible is used by some to condone the death penalty, to keep women subservient to men, to incite Islamophobia...' In his 2013 Declaration, he wrote that claiming the Bible condemned all forms of homosexuality will become a minority view in the same way as those who cited Biblical justifications for slavery and a secondary role for women.

There are, at most, six Biblical passages commonly used to condemn same-sex relationships.

The story of Sodom and Gomorrah (Genesis 19) has nothing to say on the subject: it is actually about gang-rape. No Old Testament or Apocryphal reference to Sodom and Gomorrah interpret their sin as having to do with homosexuality (Isaiah 1:10, 3:9; Jeremiah 23:14; etc.) The same is true for the one Gospel reference in Luke 10:10-12.

Two verses in Leviticus (18:22 and 20:13) complete the sum total of what the Old Testament says about same-sex activities. They do not refer to sexual orientation; they're about a married man having sex with another man (instead of his wife). Renowned public theologian Martin Marty asks conservatives 'Do you take these prohibitions literally?' As the answer is usually 'yes', he follows with another question: 'And what about the penalty: "they shall be put to death"'? (The term 'abomination' is also used of married couples having sex while the wife is menstruating; eating pork, etc). Remember that Leviticus (25:35-38) also forbids lending money at interest: our (Christian) attitude now is that the interest should not be excessive...

In the New Testament, we have three passages by Paul: the first two list a group of people who won't 'inherit the Kingdom' if they don't change: (a) 1 Corinthians 6:9-10 (the Greek word *malakoi* refers to a widespread ancient repugnance with the idea of a man taking a female role); (b) 1 Timothy 1:10: Scholars here debate the meaning of *arsenokoites*. It's unlikely Paul had a concept of sexual orientation in mind; and he certainly was not describing a committed adult relationship. (c) In Romans 1:26-27, Paul condemns swapping one's marriage partner for one of the same gender.

Summary: Paul certainly does not have any idea of same-sex orientation: he's simply giving his imprimatur to the distrust Jews living in a Graeco-Roman world had about erotic partnerships between people - male or female - who practised same-sex activity.

3. FOLLOWING JESUS TO THE MARGINALISED

Australian Anglican scholar Rev. Dr Keith Mascord and many others have decried the 'acrimonious and damaging debate...' (about same-sex marriage) 'which they surely knew was certain to cause widespread suffering to some of Australia's most vulnerable citizens. Even a small amount of research would have revealed high levels of suicide, self-harm, and mental health vulnerability among those whose lives, relationships, identity, and worth would become the subject of public debate... [Opponents of same-sex marriage] are scaring ignorant Christians into 'thinking that society will unravel if marriage is extended to include LGBTI-plus Australians.'

'The strategy is dishonest in arguing that children will become the innocent victims of a "yes" outcome... All available evidence suggests that children brought up by same-sex couples do equally well as those brought up by opposite sex couples...' [4]

In an *Open Letter to the Anglican Diocese of Sydney* [Google it], Keith announces he accepted the position of National Chaplain at Mission Australia - a 'compassionate work'.

And in the best article I've ever read on this subject: Dr David Gushee argues that the Church throughout its history has persecuted Jews, and we've used the same arguments to ostracise LGBTI people.

4. BEING GAY, BEING CHRISTIAN: YOU CAN BE BOTH

... is the title of an excellent book by Dr Stuart Edser (Australian gay Christian academic, psychologist). Stuart presents a compelling case for tolerance and acceptance, rejecting the traditional Christian view that gay people are sick or sinful as a result of their sexual orientation. Another two excellent books are Matthew Vines' *God and the Gay Christian: the Biblical Case in Support of Same-Sex Relationships* and *Justin Lee's Torn: Rescuing the Gospel from the Gays-vs.-Christians Debate*.

5. CHURCHES OUGHT TO WELCOME LGBTI CHRISTIANS.

Here you can Google my articles on this subject on *jmm.org.au* including my review of the Evangelical Alliance's *Beyond Stereotypes*. I would also recommend Yvette Flunder (a black pastor who attacks heteroprivilege in churches); Rev. Matt Glover (Australian Baptist pastor, counsellor) 'A Pastoral Response...'; Timothy Kurek (a straight guy who pretended to be gay for a year) and Andrew Marin (straight young Evangelical who did what Jesus did...).

6. WHAT CAN ONE PERSON DO... ???

People who've been marginalised because of who they are may become defensive. They don't need interrogating, but friendship. But if they sense they're in a safe place, if they feel included and are accepted for who they are, they might trust someone with their story. But it will happen at their time, at their pace. And if they can find a caring friend who will not be judgmental, and who has the prayerfully-honed skill of 'simply listening' rather than probing for secrets that their friend is not ready to share, you might be surprised at how a marginalised human being responds to such caring sensitivity. 'If I have faith, enough to move mountains, but do not have love, I am nothing' (1 Corinthians 15:2). (And, finally, note that intrusive questioning about one's sexual practices are almost always inappropriate: leave that to counsellors and medicos...)

A modern ethicist and theologian, Fuller Seminary's Professor Lew Smedes used to teach several decades ago that we should 'Treat marriage equality as we did divorce'.

Ex-Pentecostal Australian Evangelist Anthony Venn-Brown's best-seller, A Life of Unlearning has an excellent – and frank – autobiography of a married preacher-and-father of two daughters, who's 'come out of the closet'. His slogan: 'We're here. We're Queer. We Believe!'

Finally, a memo to myself

1. One of my primary callings is to do what Jesus did: befriend the marginalised. A despised Samaritan - not the clergy - helped the wounded Jew on the road-side.

Back in the 1970s, when I was something of a Pharisee (don't take offence; I'm describing myself), I thought I was pleasing God by telling gays to change: or else live a life of lonely celibacy (and be excluded from any significant ministry in the church). 'If you see some brother or sister in need and have the means to do something about it but turn cold shoulder and do nothing, what happens to God's love? It disappears. And you made it disappear' (1 John 3:16-17, *The Message* version).

2. Then about 30 years ago, I began hearing too many stories of gay peoples' awful pain - sometimes rejected even by their Christian families when they 'came out'. If teenagers, they had four or five times more chance of committing suicide than their non-gay friends.

3. In the past few decades, scientific bodies began legitimising LGBTI's experience; decades of research and clinical experience have all led mainstream mental health organisations in the US/Western nations to the conclusion that homosexuality is a normal form of human sexuality. Many recent scientific studies reveal a strong biological component to being gay (perhaps a better term than 'genetic' because, though the trait is innate, it is not explained by genes alone). Homosexuality is a congenital condition much like being left-handed. Remember back in your history when being left-handed meant you were possessed by an evil spirit? Scientific beliefs change as we gain new

information, and sometimes science tells us things we would rather not hear. Get used to it.

4. The church has sometimes-to-often changed its mind: the earth isn't the centre of the universe; race/slavery/miscegenation (most recently in Nazi Germany, Apartheid in South Africa, the US South); Jews are not now called Christ-killers; accepting divorcees etc. The doyen of public theologians, Martin Marty: 'The gay rights movement has achieved more swiftly than any other rights movement in history, not merely the impossible but the unthinkable'.

5. Two 'aha' moments. I was being interviewed live on ABCTV by the genial Peter Couchman with two women from the prostitutes' collective, when out of the blue one of them turned to me and asked 'Why do you Christians hate us?' I mumbled something like 'I don't hate anyone'. But that night I resigned from the Festival of Light. Second, my cumulative research from counselling people for marriage revealed that about 95-97% of them were, technically, 'fornicators'; they were not virgins. But those people were not barred from public church ministries. Heterosexual sin before/outside marriage is apparently OK, but not homosexual sex - or even simply a same-sex orientation. (I remember outlining that hypocrisy to a Sydney-based ABCTV team. When I asked why they came to Melbourne to interview me they said: 'We can't find any Progressive Evangelical Church Leaders in Sydney on these questions!')

6. I've been privileged to travel widely ministering to overseas missionaries. They often took me aside to confess their sins/issues. Like the mature woman who masturbated accompanied by visions of have a same-sex experience with another woman. Like the two woman who lived together in the same missionary-cottage, and who were bisexual...

7. The sins listed in Romans 1:26, 1 Corinthians 6:9, etc. do not refer to life-long loving unions between same-sex couples.

8. Progressives (I'm happy to be named in that group, so long as Evangelical is in there somewhere) tend to be guided by a higher commitment to grace rather than ancient practices or law or dogma, as they believe Jesus was with his ethic of inclusion. Many family-members have changed their mind when a loved one 'comes out' as gay. (What's new, ask progressive apologists: the same thing happened with the inter-racial and divorce paradigms.)

9. Luther and Calvin both challenged the theological norm of their day that marriage was first for the procreation of children. Rather, they posited, God had provided a way out of human loneliness via the calling to a lifelong, committed relationship. (Jesus' and Paul's recorded words never connected the institution of marriage with procreation.)

10. How did humans learn to discriminate against certain individuals/groups? René Girard has been most helpful here with his notion of mimetic rivalry: humans learn bigotry from parents/significant others. Society is believed to be at risk from 'alien others', so they must be opposed/humiliated/punished/exiled... even killed. In other words, these alien individuals or outgroups become 'scapegoats' in a society's quest for purity, salvation, orthodoxy, whatever.

Conclusion: Jesus is the ultimate revelation of God, and other parts of Scripture must be interpreted through Jesus and his teachings. For example, in the Old Testament, we read that God commanded Joshua to kill every man, woman and child in the city of Jericho: let us interpret that in the light of the teaching of Jesus to love one's enemies. The teaching/example of Jesus takes precedence over all other ideologies.

Endnotes

[1] *The Melbourne Anglican*, December 2018, p. 13.
[2] The Sunday Age, 16 September 2018, p. 2.
[3] Google Chalke, LGBT article by Alex Williams, 27 Jan 2018
[4] Google Rev. Dr Keith Mascord 'Churches who campaigned for "no" 7 November 2017'

Chapter 7
FATHER ROD BOWERS: AUSTRALIA'S BEST-KNOWN CONTEMPORARY POPULAR PROPHET

He came to fame in July 2013, with a provocative roadside sign outside his parish church in Gosford, N.S.W.:

SOME PPL ARE GAY
GET OVER IT
LOVE GOD

Four years later, it helped his nation to vote for marriage equality by more than 60%. Australia has held 44 public referendums to change the constitution and only seven produced a higher national vote...

The story behind this slogan? He'd been asked to give the last rites to a gay man, and the family apparently assumed that a Sydney-area Anglican clergyman wouldn't approve of the man's partner sharing the sacrament. 'I wanted to put out a clear message to the community that if you're gay or lesbian you're welcome here.' He has the view that Jesus would have agreed, but unfortunately the church has often (mostly?) separated the message from the medium. Jesus' most accepting audience was not only a poor marginalised people, oppressed by the Romans, but also – religiously – by the dogma of the religious clergy of his day.

'And when you separate the two this message becomes about getting people into heaven, rather than getting heaven into people' he told a reporter from the Melbourne *Age* newspaper. [1]

Rod says his activism is informed by having the perspective of the outsider, which has come from his being adopted. Although loved and wanted by his adoptive parents, he sees other families as an outsider looking in. Even in senior church staff meetings, 'I still feel as if I don't belong. I tend to choose justice over order. I don't want to abandon order, but I think order without justice is tyranny...' He backs up his argument by citing Martin Luther King who said the real danger he faced came 'not so much from the Ku Klux Klan but the white moderates who preferred order over justice.' Father Rod's other great hero is Dom Helder Camara, the Brazilian Catholic archbishop whose most famous quote was: "When I give food to the poor, they call me a saint. When I ask why are they poor, they call me a Communist". [2]

Back to Rod's adoptive family. He has good and bad memories of the man whose last words as he lay dying were to ask for his cigarettes. 'He was an alcoholic and there were some terrifying times. He would wave firearms around when he was drunk. When he was sober, he was a gentle, decent man.' [Ibid]. Rod had two mothers to make up for the loss of his father– his adoptive mother (now 85) and his birth mother, only 17 years older than himself, and with whom he reconnected after a 29-year gap. The two mums have a nice, if distant, friendship.

Rod had some self-destructive years after his father died. But on Christmas Day 1984 he 'woke with a hangover from hell. Nevertheless, he decided for some reason to go to church. In his memoir, *Outspoken* [3], he wrote, 'Something stirred within me that day... another world had opened wide its arms and engulfed me. This was my introduction to Anglo-Catholicism.' He went to theological college, but confesses 'I spent more on whisky than I spent on books'.

ooOoo

In November 2018, I spent a week immersed in Rod's autobiography, and marked these sentences:

> 'I am positive that had women been ordained in Christian churches 50 years earlier, we would never have been in need of a Royal Commission into child sexual abuse. The ordination of women ushered in a revitalised culture to the clergy and to the Church, one that was much less reliant on power and more genuinely focused on love.' [p. 70]

> 'We cannot avoid the issue of power in human society... I do not want power, but I don't want anyone else to have it either. But that wish can never be a reality. In every relationship, in every organisation, in every community, in every society, someone has power. And that is never truer than in the Church.' [p. 117]

> 'For the Church to function productively in public discourse, it needs both theological orthodoxy and progressive engagement.' [p. 163]

'The Irish referendum taught us many things, one of which is that the "Church" does not oppose marriage equality; the institution of the Church may, some bishops and leaders may, some doctrinal gatekeepers may, some Christians may, but the majority of the Irish people did not, and the majority of Irish people identify as Christian. The Church, after all, in its purist definition, is the people... In Australia, as in Ireland, the majority of Christians ignored their institutional leaders and doctrinal gatekeepers and supported marriage equality; they blessed and affirmed and said Yes!' [pp. 200, 201]

'I join with Martin Luther King Jr. echoing the voice of the prophet Amos (5:24), who puts these words into the mouth of God: "I have no interest in your wealth or your words but let justice roll down like waters, and righteousness like an ever-flowing stream".' [p. 235]

'I'm not saying there's anything wrong with capitalism – it has brought great things to modern society – but when it dominates and excludes and robs the poor and oppresses the marginalised, then there is something wrong.' [p. 313]

'The offering of sanctuary to someone fleeing persecution has a long and venerable tradition in the Judeo/Christian world. The ancient principle goes back to the Hebrew Scriptures and was enshrined in English common law. In the Middle Ages, Benedictine monks set a watchman at night to make sure anyone who sought protection would be received into their midst.' [p. 328]

ooOoo

His future? Possibly standing as an independent for the Australian Senate. He has no problems combining his Christianity with politics. 'The Islamophobes talk about Islam not being a religion but a political ideology, but Christianity is a political ideology in the very same way. The whole basis of Christianity is based on an alternative kingdom with an alternative king - if that is not a political ideology I don't know what is. Jesus was executed for sedition.'

As an activist, Bower says he has three primary areas of concern. He can tick off the first, marriage equality. Next is refugees and asylum seekers, and then climate: 'It is the ultimate issue for us'. [4]

He has no doubts he'll continue to be in the firing line on all three issues. In an interview with *The Melbourne Anglican,* he said: '[We] need prophetic voices. The three hallmarks of the Hebrew prophetic tradition are: you have to be absolutely clear about what you are saying, you have to be prepared to live on the outskirts of your society or your organisation, and you have to at times be willing to be outrageous.' [5]

An example of the latter: he had to apologise for some 'offensive' remarks likening Australian offshore processing of asylum-seekers as the first step on the way to the Holocaust. Letters to newspaper editors complained strongly against his drawing this analogy 'so ignorantly and insensitively.' 'Rod Bower is right up there with those who would welcome people who hate us. No other explanation makes sense as to why the worst crime in modern history can be equated to the benign conditions on a Pacific island. But trashing the memory of those who were victims of a real Holocaust is clearly insufficient reason for Bower to miss a grandstanding opportunity to demonstrate his sick hubris.'

Rod Bower met with Jewish leaders over all this, and apologised for any 'offence' his remarks might have caused: 'I acknowledge my attempt to explore this issue was clumsy and I am sorry for the offence caused.' The chief executive of the NSW Jewish Board of Deputies, Vic Alhadeff, said he was pleased with this outcome... [6]

Rod Bower is a modern prophet in the biblical sense: he's speaking the truth in love, (though, yes, his language is sometimes 'in your face').

May his tribe increase!

Endnotes

[1] *The Age Spectrum*, 15 December 2018, p. 4.

[2] Ibid. For more on Camara, see my 2018 book *Questions & Responses 1*, chapter 7, pp. 68ff.

[3] *Outspoken: The Life and Work of the Man Behind Those Signs*, Ebury Press, 2018

[4] *Spectrum*, ibid.

[5] *The Melbourne Anglican*, October 2018, p. 11.
[6] *The Weekend Australian*, 5-6 January 2019, p. 23.

Chapter 8
DEALING WITH HATE

A troubled parishioner came to see me about a deep problem she had with another woman whom she felt was trying to seduce her husband. Her question: 'I hear you preaching regularly about the "healing power of love". Please help me to do something with my hatred for this other woman.' I listened to her story about the background to it all, and how she and her husband had tried to get help from a counsellor but he felt it wasn't helping. Then we decided to take a major foray into the meaning of hate, and how to get that issue into perspective.

Maybe your issue with hate has a different intensity or a different object. As I write, just two days ago I saw the new movie *The Australian Dream*, about white vs. Aboriginal issues in our country. It's the Adam Goodes story: he's an aboriginal AFL Brownlow Medal footballer and 2014 Australian of the Year who was heckled by the crowd (and called an 'ape' by a 13-year-old girl, who when Goodes pointed her out was escorted away by Security). The movie's narrator is the Aboriginal scholar Stan Grant, who adapted his excellent *Quarterly Essay* publication on the theme for this task. The message: we in Australia have done the reconciliation process very poorly, compared with other nations (like Canada and New Zealand). We're still primitive when it comes to dealing with our history of conquest and hate...

Slowly read this potpourri of wisdom from many sources and mark the sentences that might provide some prayerful help:

First, who said this? 'Others may hate you - but they don't win unless you hate them - and then you destroy yourself.' (Yes, you guessed it - or did you? - it was US President Richard Nixon.)

And think about this: Leonardo da Vinci felt so deeply bitter towards a rival, that he determined to use the face of that painter as his portrait of Judas. But when he then tried to paint the face of Jesus he couldn't get anywhere. He came to the conclusion that the frustration he was suffering was because of his continuing hatred of his enemy...

One of America's most famous and destructive hate-feuds was between the Hatfields and the McCoys. Somewhere between 20 and 60 were killed in the feud. Randolph McCoy lost five of his nine sons; in the ensuing reprisals, two Hatfields were killed, two were hanged, and seven jailed.

Some thoughts to ponder:

* 'Words of hate leave footprints in the mind' (Franz Kafka).

* 'It's much easier to turn hate into love than to turn fear into love' (Christopher Isherwood).

* Bertrand Russell was supposed to have said that most people could not be really happy unless they hated some other person, nation or creed.

* 'Hatred is always more damaging to the vessel in which it is stored, than the object on which it is poured.'

* Do you enjoy the pain that others you don't like experience? Here's an observation from a 19th century colonial newspaper: 'A dentist with a toothache is a spectacle as rare as it is gratifying. It comes perhaps but once in a lifetime, but it brings with it a fragrance that lingers for years.'

* One New Year's Eve, a lady was riding her bicycle along a beautiful treed road, when some male voices from a passing car shouted, 'Ride, you fat bitch!' She said later: 'I was shocked, and deeply wounded. They weren't to know that I was riding to lose weight. And I'm not a female dog...' She went on: 'Race, religion, body-shape, intelligence, and even where one lives can be the subject of taunts that leave psychological scars.'

* Nine-year-old Erika Delgado was the sole survivor of a plane crash that took the lives of 52 people, including her mother, father and younger brother, outside Cartagena in Colombia on 11 January 1995. She found herself in a bed of algae and water lilies, suffering from fractures and pneumonia. Someone, ignoring her cries for help, ripped a gold necklace from her neck and ran away. Scavengers looted the bodies of the other passengers... [1]

ooOoo

In August 1990, Elie Wiesel exercised his moral authority by bringing together an astonishing collection of Nobel Prize Winners and world political leaders for a 'Hate Conference'. 'Hate is difficult' wrote Lance Morrow in a *Time* Essay: 'The subject is amorphous, disorderly, malignant'. Presiding over the sessions, Elie Wiesel controlled a red light on the podium to warn a speaker when their time was up (even President Carter got red-lighted)... What is hate? A 'black sun', Wiesel wrote. It's a cretin with a club, violent, repulsive, irrational, a black intoxication, an accomplice of death... If there were any haters there, they kept their secret. The major controversy was between objectivists and subjectivists. The subjectivists (poets and moralists) looked for hatred within the human heart. The objectivists (economists, historians, lawyers) located the causes of hatred in the conditions of people's lives... [2]

In another *Time* essay [3] Pico Iyer wrote: As he was writing wartime propaganda for the British government, Graham Greene described an Englishman's shooting of a German lieutenant – and then finding in the dead man's pocket a picture of his baby. Greene made it his lifework to understand every position: one of his plays is even called "Yes and No"... As he put it in *The Power and the Glory*: "When you visualised a man or a woman carefully, you could always begin to feel pity... When you saw the corners of the eyes, the shape of the mouth, how the hair grew, it was impossible to hate. Hate was just a failure of imagination... The most sobering lesson of Greene's fiction is that sleeping with the enemy is most with us when we're sleeping alone..."

When I was an English teacher, one of the books on school reading lists was William Golding's *Lord of the Flies*, which depicts brilliantly the cruelty with which children afflict one another. Another teacher wrote: 'With the framework of civilised society removed, some, like Ralph and Piggy, continue to adhere to its rules and guiding principles, whereas others, like Jack and his henchman Roger, use it as an opportunity to indulge their baser instincts. The weak are quickly bullied and outcast, the vulnerable manipulated, the different humiliated and destroyed. Most terrifying of all, however, is how the more sensible of the boys idolise the adult world of sense and order, fairness and safety, when the whole reason why they are on the island in the first place is because the adults are all at war with one another, and what is happening on the island is a mere microcosm of what is taking place on the battlefields of WWII'. [4]

Can you legislate against hatred? Australia's 1994 *Race Hatred Bill* included three new race-hate crimes, which are committed by (1) making threats to cause physical harm or (2) damaging property or (3) inciting others to racial hatred - if those incitements are committed because of race, ethnicity or nationality. Every element of each offence must be proved beyond reasonable doubt...

What makes holocaust deniers tick? (Problem: the youngest survivors of the camps are now in their mid-to-late eighties). Eminent holocaust author Professor Deborah Lipstadt: 'Haters are tenacious and they teach their children to hate... More people believe that Elvis is alive than that the holocaust did not happen'. [5]

From an article on 'The Cultivation of Hatred': 'Every culture develops its distinctive strategies for the handling of aggression. Racism, sexism, nationalism, imperialism: these are some of the time-honoured rationalisations that serve to cultivate hate... 19th century modernity was a product of aggression - exploitative, degenerate, alienated and destructive. Yet it was also an age in which the cultivation of hatred was pressed into the service of creativity and renewal... Individuals and classes, races and nations are divided into insiders and outsiders'. [6]

Where's the most hate per capita in our world? Try this: When the UN's man in Sarajevo back in the early 1990s, General Lewis MacKenzie, was asked how that area compared with others – Gaza, Nicaragua, Cyprus and other peace-keeping tours – he said: 'You can take the hate from all those previous tours and multiply by ten... Here it's grown to horrendous proportions. If the leadership said "OK let's sit down and sort this thing out", I'm not sure whether people would accept that because there is so much hate for the other side/s. Really deep, gut-wrenching hate. Once you start calling them baby killers, pregnant-women killers, and talk about cooking babies, those are not good grounds for negotiations'. [7]

Some politicians actually say they develop hating attitudes. Ros Kelly said, as she left the Australian Federal Parliament's front bench, that she was a good 'hater' (!), and politician-cum-political commentator Graham Richardson proved he was, in his autobiography.

The role of envy: In a *Time* essay titled 'Why Writers Attack Writers', Truman Capote on Jack Kerouac: 'That's not writing, it's typing.' Gore Vidal on Capote: 'He made lying an art. A minor art.' Novelist J. G. Cozzens, perhaps expressing sour grapes of wrath: 'I cannot read ten pages of Steinbeck without throwing up'. [8]

Why do many people hate Jews? Perhaps this quote has something to do with it: 'In the U.S. Jews constitute barely 2 percent of the population, but they account for close to half its billionaires, for the leadership of all three major television networks... for the ownership of the nation's largest chain of newspapers and for considerable percentages of university faculties'. [9]

WHAT POSITIVE ANTIDOTES TO HATE CAN WE LEARN?

A potpourri of wisdom from people who've learned some wisdom:

- ❖ The opposite of love is not hatred, but indifference.
- ❖ Booker T. Washington said: 'I will not permit anyone to degrade my soul by making me hate him'.
- ❖ The spirit of forgiveness is essential to our mental, emotional, spiritual and physical health. We all know folks who harbour resentment and animosity for decades and wondered why life seemed so jaundiced to them.
- ❖ Someone said to a Jewish scholar: 'Your Bible - our Old Testament - is full of hate!' 'No,' he said. '"Peace" gets 237 mentions, "love" 231, and "hate" has 129'.

WHAT CAN WE DO TO HEAL OUR HATRED/S?

First, realise...

'People with clenched fists cannot shake hands'. If we are full of hatred and anger we quickly destroy all relationships around us. Forgiveness for many is a lovely idea until they have something to forgive.

'To give someone else a piece of your mind is to lose your own peace of mind.'

Then: practise forgiving:

'To err is human, to forgive divine. The only petition in the Lord's Prayer with a condition attached to it is the one on forgiveness.'

'We are like beasts when we kill (and that includes character assassination). We are human when we judge. We are like God when we forgive.'

- ❖ 'Forgiveness is the key that unlocks the door of resentment and the handcuffs of hate. It breaks the chains of bitterness and the shackles of selfishness.'
- ❖ St Paul (Ephesians 4:31-32): 'Get rid of all bitterness, passion and anger. No more shouting or insults, no more hateful feelings of any sort. Instead, be kind and tenderhearted to one another, and forgive one another, as God has forgiven you through Christ'.
- ❖ Chrysostom: 'Nothing causes us to so nearly resemble God as the forgiveness of injuries.'
- ❖ Is hatred of anything ever appropriate? Yes: 'You that love the Lord, hate evil' (Psalm 97:10).

ooOoo

And now a little homily by Richard Rohr in one of his daily devotions: 'The ego is that part of the self that wants to be significant, central and important by itself, apart from anybody else. It wants to be both separate and superior. It is defended and self-protective by its very nature. It must eliminate the negative to succeed at this. The ego is what Jesus called an "actor," usually translated from the Greek as "hypocrite" (see Matthew 23).

'If our "actor" is merely defended, the shadow will be denied and repressed; but if our "actor" is over-defended, the shadow is actually hated and projected elsewhere (for example, there are often homosexual ministers who hate and attack homosexuals). One point here is crucial: The shadow self is not of itself evil: it just allows you to do evil without recognising it as evil! That is why Jesus criticises hypocrisy more than anything else. Jesus is not upset with sinners, but only with people who pretend they are not sinners... The cause of our unrecognised and fully operative evil is our egocentricity, not our weaknesses. Jesus opposes the sins of malice with which he has no patience... The root cause is our over-defended ego, which always sees, hates, and attacks its own faults in other people, and thus avoids its own conversion.' [10]

Back to the lady who hates the other woman who's trying to seduce her husband. What wisdom do we have for her?

It's not simple, but here are a few angles on it all:

1. Consider this quote from an abandoned wife: 'They were so caught up in each other that it justified their

behaviour. And who knows what he told her? He can tell her anything. She probably thinks she is rescuing him!'

2. Some advice from a Psychologist:

2-1. Stop using dirty words to refer to the other woman. It feels good for the moment, but brings you down in some psychic way, if only to yourself.

2-2. Stop asking about the details of the affair; he just may be tempted to tell you.

2-3. Recognise that most husbands who've had long-term affairs have told the other woman that the marriage is virtually over, and that "my wife knows it". He lies to you, and he lies to her too.

2-4. Exercise discipline. As soon as you can manage it, stop checking her Facebook page, stop asking everyone about her, stop stalking her. It makes you look bad and feel worse.

2-5. Don't try to meet with the other woman; nothing good that will come of it.

2-6. Turn down the volume on her importance in your life. Unless she was a friend, this is really about you and him.

2-7. Be kind to yourself! [11]

What's missing – from a Christian perspective – in those seven suggestions?

It's complicated, and you can't generalise from a specific situation to all others. Briefly, as a pastor, I'd be asking her whether she was OK about my seeing her husband? Then I'd be seeing them both separately and together, if they were open to all that. Perhaps out of that, depending on the state of their desire to reconcile they could be advised to see a good marriage counsellor (even though they tried that once before).

Of course, if she's a church member and he isn't, there's usually a big complication there...

Finally...

'If someone says "I love God" but hates another Christian, that person is a liar; for if we don't love people we can see, how can we love God, whom we have not seen? And God himself has commanded that we must love not only him but our Christian brothers and sisters, too.' 1 John 4:20-21 (*The Message* version)

'Hatred stirs up quarrels, but love covers all offences.' Proverbs 10:12

'You have heard that the law of Moses says, 'Love your neighbour' and hate your enemies. But I say, love your enemy! Pray for those who persecute you! In that way, you will be acting as true children of your Father in heaven. For he gives his sunlight to both the evil and the good, and he sends rain on the just and on the unjust too.' Matthew 5:43-44.

'Forgive one another, as God in Christ forgave you' Ephesians 4:32.

Endnotes

[1]   *Time*, 30 January 1995, p. 10.
[2]   Google the article – *Time*, September 1990, for more
[3]   *Time*, 20 February 1995.
[4]   https://bookssnob.wordpress.com/2012/08/30/lord-

of-the-flies-by-william-golding/

[5] 'Denying the Holocaust: the Growing Assault on Truth and Memory'. *The Australian*, 22 July 1994, p. 7.

[6] Anthony Elliott, 'The Cultivation of Hatred' by Peter Gay, *Weekend Review*, July 23-24, 1994, p. 6.

[7] *Time*, 17 August 1992, pp. 25-26.

[8] *Time*, 24 January 2000, p. 66.

[9] *Christian Century*, 29 June 1996, p. 662.

[10] Things Hidden: Scripture as Spirituality, 2008, 75-76

[11] https://www.psychologytoday.com/au/blog/schlepping-through-heartbreak/201711/the-other-woman-s-role-in-your-breakup

Chapter 9
CREATIVITY AND RELIGIOUS INSTITUTIONS: A POTPOURRI OF WISDOM

1. YOUR CHURCH CAN COME ALIVE: THE BASICS

First, a *disclosure*: I am writing this chapter primarily as a pastor to my fellow-pastors. You may not be a pastor/minister/priest, but if you're a committed Christian, I would encourage you to read it all anyway, and mark a few sections to share (respectfully) with your church's leader/s.

Your first question to me ought to be: 'Rowland, what do you know about leading a church to significant health and growth?' Good question: thanks for asking. I don't usually talk about this from a personal perspective, but feel that I should here offer some history and credentials. Fasten your seat-belts: there will be some turbulence!

Some *biographical background:* I have led the pastoral team as the resident senior pastoral leader in five churches/ Christian groups.

Chronologically: first, the Christian Fellowship group at Bathurst Teachers' College, 1958 (of which I was president). An unusual thing happened there: a majority of the male students in my year – except for those who were Catholics or secularists – were already or became committed Christians, and the weekly Christian Fellowship experienced what some have called 'a mini-revival'. That's a story for another day.

Then, after five years as a secondary school teacher (during which I completed by correspondence a B.A. degree with the University of New England), I felt called to apply for the Baptist ministry. I did the four-year course at what is now termed Morling (Baptist) College in Sydney, and also was part-time student-pastor at Narwee Baptist Church for those four years. That church – following Ken Manley's three years ministry (visit his story in another chapter in this book) – had a solid foundation for growth, and following a two year ministry by another friend, Bill Leng (who became later Vice-Principal of the Melbourne Bible Institute), we were called to lead one of the two happiest churches I've ever known. There were many baptisms, the congregation doubled in size, growing to nearly 100 members, and the staff also grew by the addition of a full-time youth pastor (Dave Kendall) and a part-time deaconess. Also the missionary emphasis grew, until within a few years it had the largest budget for overseas missions of any Baptist church in NSW. Now student pastorates are not supposed to do all that, the theory being that I was primarily dedicated to mastering the Bible, theology, history, Baptist Principles, New Testament Greek, etc. and the pastorate was there to 'ground' me in the Baptist ethos, etc.

Upon graduation and ordination, guess what? The Bathurst 'revival' had been talked about amongst the leaders of the Intervarsity Fellowship, and they invited me to travel Australia as a Staffworker, encouraging about 40 or so Christian groups in various tertiary institutions. So I may have been, to that point, the only Baptist College graduate ordained to a ministry, not to a missionary appointment overseas, or another pastoral ministry in a church, but as a wandering prophet for three years full-time, and two years part-time, to the tertiary institutions of our nation. There were many counselling, leadership training, and speaking opportunities (including a week's mission at the University of Sydney)...

During those five years I also did a Masters Degree in Educational Psychology at the University of Sydney. One dramatic discovery was worth that whole educational experience. It was a one-sentence summary of an amazing truism by sociologist Robert Merton, which I'd never heard before, but actually practised in the limited opportunities I'd had so far in pastoral leadership. Are you ready for it? 'Individuals mostly increase their commitment to an ideology to the degree that they are encouraged to verbalise that commitment.' IOW (in other words), there ought always to be regular opportunities for those who are led to spend their lives spreading the good news (about a political or religious ideology or whatever) to talk with other trainees and potential converts about their belief-system...

Now a corollary of that truism is that pastors ought to encourage people to study and master the Christian faith and life – mostly perhaps in small groups – with a view to being competent in evangelism and the encouragement of spiritual growth of their converts. It's what they did in the dynamic New Testament churches. But guess what? The evils of clericalism have meant that it's professional clergy who do most of the verbalising of the faith in church meetings. In most churches the so-called 'laity' don't get much of a chance to do it, nor do most church services encourage people - openly - to ask questions. And so the census statistics in Australia tell the story: most mainline churches and denominations are rapidly declining. [1]

I once did a hands-up survey in a large Eastern States clergy conference where I was the invited speaker. 'Hands up', I asked them, 'if you know of one mainline church in Eastern Australia which is growing significantly, but they still have a predictable liturgy, same-old hymns etc., the pastor does most of the preaching, and there are no opportunities for questions...?' In all of Eastern Australia, only two or three churches got a mention. What was unique about them? They had a very gifted preaching communicator whose sermonic skills overcame the 'drag' of those other variables...

The final fifteen of those months included a part-time interim ministry at Central Baptist Church in Sydney (Australia's first Baptist Church): it was an exciting time, and the congregations grew until the balcony was comfortably filled towards the end of our 15 months there. But a small group of conservatives didn't appreciate our bringing the congregation into the present era, and they stacked a meeting called by the deacons to invite us to stay as senior pastor, with people who hadn't been attending, and I missed out on the required 75% by about two votes...

Meanwhile, other invitations-to-ministry had come our way, and we resigned our membership at CBC. [2] What now followed is the most exciting marriage of a church-and-pastor I have ever experienced. My next appointment was for nearly eight years' senior pastor of what became Australia's largest

Baptist Church (Blackburn, Victoria). It's an exciting story, but here are the headlines:

We called associate pastoral staff before we could afford them. My strong conviction – it had already happened at Narwee – was that 'the money would follow'. Those gifted pastors wrote their own ministry descriptions. We encouraged them to work within their areas of giftedness – I did not attend one single Finance Committee meeting in eight years – but they were also encouraged to disciple others… We trained lay leaders: our church became essentially about 60 home groups who met during the week for Bible study, prayer, and *koinonia*, and came together on Sundays.

When I met with the 'call committee' to discuss being invited to 'BBC', they asked, among other things, what I might do with the evening service? My response: 'People aren't generally interested in coming to another service which is similar to the morning ones. I've been working with students for several years, and you've got to invite questions to get their interest. And the music should be mostly contemporary. Remember it's a television age. At Central Baptist Church, we saw the church fill up – with students and nurses. Trust me with all that'. And it happened. Of the 1000 or more attending the three services most Sundays, the evening service was the most dynamic – though the 'family services' in the morning also had an important/alternative mode of corporate worship. There's much more, of course: 'Crossway' as that church came to be called, now has about 5000 attending: still easily the largest Baptist Church ever in Australia. [3]

2. CREATIVITY AND BUREAUCRACY: Random notes from many seminars

* Both apples and oranges have their place; but no matter how hard you squeeze an apple, you just won't get orange juice... Bureaucracy without creativity leads to jokes about political/civil servants...

* A popular theory is that we are either left-brained or right-brained, meaning that one side of our brain is dominant. If you're mostly analytical and methodical in your thinking, you're said to be left-brained. If you tend to be more creative or artistic, you're right-brained. This theory was developed in the 1960s, thanks to the research of psychobiologist and Nobel Prize winner Roger W. Sperry. Humans being what they are will despise either the bureaucratic mindset of the left-brained person, or the artistic mindset of those who are right-brained.

* In the Spirituality seminars I've attended, I've often heard the theory that those who get into positions of power in the church usually do not have a well-developed spiritual life. Spirituality is about the transformation of people; this takes time the bureaucrat mostly doesn't have. 'Power corrupts, and absolute power corrupts absolutely.' The classic analysis of bureaucracy by sociologist Max Weber involved his theory about a special form of corruption: the cult of expertise.

* I remember the late 1980s as an era when creativity became a buzzword for Western businesses. John Sanford bemoans the trend of churches becoming increasingly institutionalised. 'In putting the life of the institution above that of the soul, it lost the dream; instead of ministering and listening to the soul, the church has sought to mould the individual to the life of the institution.' [4]

* But of all the New Testament churches, the Corinthian congregation proves to us that institutional power need not necessarily be viewed as the enemy of creativity. Paul had to plead for order to preserve the essence of the church's life.

* Creative thinking is many-faceted. Heard of the guy who made a little yellow banner with the words John 3:16 on it and traveled to many sporting events around the world displaying it? Millions on TV saw it, and many commentators actually looked it up and recited those famous words. Not a bad return for his efforts to educate the world with the greatest news humankind has ever heard, eh?

* You are captured by terrorists. The fanatical leader tells you that if you make a truthful statement he will shoot you, but if you make a false statement you will die slowly by a thousand cuts. After a little thought you come up with a statement that results in the puzzled leader setting you free. What was that simple

statement? It was: 'I will die by a thousand cuts'.

* There was a UK petrol shortage in April 1979. The Government imposed a ten pound *maximum* on petrol purchases. Result: motorists went from pump to pump filling up, resulting in a nation of drivers with full or near full petrol tanks – and eventually none at the petrol pumps. The Irish? They imposed a ten pound *minimum*: so they drove around until they were nearly empty – and *plenty* of petrol at the pumps. One Irishman observed: 'We may be slightly insane... but we're not stupid'.

* Do you have some of traits of creative problem-solving? Notice which are answered true or false:

1. You were closer to your mother than to your father. True
2. You have always been a good reader. True
3. You daydream more than your friends do. True
4. The more intelligent you are, the more imaginative and creative you are likely to be. False
5. Since our IQs are limited, we cannot increase our problem-solving ability. False
6. It is always easier to solve a problem if you are eager to do so. False
7. It's best to strongly focus all your attention on your problem and try to think it through. False
8. It's best to be under some degree of stress when trying to solve a problem. True

9. Building confidence through repeated success will always increase your ability to be a good problem solver. False
10. To be creative we must apply consistent effort to our problems. False. [5]

* What did Roosevelt and Gorbachev have in common? Roosevelt re society's problems: 'The country needs bold, persistent experimentation: if it fails, try something else'. Gorbachev reckoned Soviet domination of Eastern Europe was a drag on his campaign to restructure the Soviet Union. Hence his emergence as the Commissar Liberator. He adopted many of the West's favourite buzz words: stability, mutual security, the unwinnability of nuclear war, interdependence, human values and a civil society.

* Heard about the man who invented a fail-safe repellant that led to starlings and pigeons hot-footing it off buildings? People had tried rubber snakes, stuffed owls, electric wires, metal spikes, and lots more. But then entrepreneur Roger Snow developed a cartridge gun which sprayed a surface with a sticky substance. Birds had momentary trouble taking off, so they gave out distress cries which deterred other birds from approaching... Simple, eh?

* Seminaries and churches can focus all their instruction on subjects like church dogma, rituals, rites and rules. Jesus didn't. He favoured a heart seeking God

over strict rules: teachers-of-rules will punish that attitude... Institutional religion anaesthetises and inoculates people, giving them just enough so that they never really walk the inner journey... They should be asking 'Am I a spiritual person, or am I just a religious person'?

* The failure of Rationalism is that it tries to find a place for God in its picture of the world. But God, whose centre is everywhere and circumference nowhere, cannot be fitted into a diagram. He is rather the canvas on which the picture is painted, or the frame in which it is set...

* A Dominican priest who majored in the area of spiritual theology, Richard Woods, was asked about mental prayer. His response: 'I discovered *mystical* prayer... by making *The Cloud of Unknowing* my spiritual guide. One of the things it teaches is to stop thinking, to stop talking, to stop everything and just be aware of God's presence... to utilise the sense of love and not to try to fathom or do anything else, just to be there. [6] I spent the best year of my life - spiritually - walking and praying, immersed in *The Cloud of Unknowing.*

Scriptures: Think on these:

Proverbs 30:18-19: 'Three things are too wonderful for me/four which I don't understand: the way of a vulture in the sky, the way of a serpent on a rock, the way of a ship out at sea, and the way of a man with a girl'.

Psalm 46:10: 'Be still and know that I am God.'

Colossians 3:15: 'Let the peace of Christ rule in your hearts, since as members of one body you were called to peace, and be thankful.'

Hebrews 12:14: 'Make every effort to live at peace with everyone, and to be holy; without holiness no one will see the Lord.'

Reinhold Niebuhr's *The Serenity Prayer:*

God grant me the serenity to accept the things I cannot
change, courage to change the things I can, and
wisdom to know the difference.

Living one day at a time;

Enjoying one moment at a time;

Accepting hardships as the pathway to peace;

Taking, as he did, this sinful world

as it is, not as I would have it;

Trusting that he will make all things right

if I surrender to his will;

That I may be reasonably happy in this life

and supremely happy with him

Forever in the next.

Amen. [7]

Grant that, this day and every day, we may keep our shock of wonder at each new beauty that comes upon us as we walk down the paths of life. Amen.

Endnotes

[1] See the three chapters titled *What Does a Healthy Church Look Like?* in Questions and Responses, Volume 2.

[2] You're asking 'What/Where was the fifth congregation? It was an 18 months' ministry in Vancouver, Canada. It requires a whole chapter another time. But for now, Google The Vancouver 'Adventure' jmm.org.au.

[3] More: See my little book *Your Church Can Come Alive*, a summary of my dissertation for a Doctor of Ministry degree at Fuller Seminary, Pasadena, U.S.A. Visit ABE books or The Book Depository online: all my out-of-print books are there from time to time.

[4] John Sanford, *Dreams and Healing*, Paulist Press, 1978, p. 8.

[5] Salvatore Didato.

[6] Interview with Richard Woods by Betty and Art Winter, Praying No.11, p. 22.

[7] https://www.whatchristianswanttoknow.com/serenity-prayer-and-7-lessons-from-it/#ixzz5qseYrzbZ

Chapter 10
RICHARD ROHR: AN APPRECIATION

Father Richard Rohr, a contemporary Franciscan theologian, pastor and teacher, is famous for giving us at least a thousand quotable quotes...
Like:

* 'Without us God will not. But without God we cannot.'

* 'Much contemporary preaching may be inspirational and even good theology, but it often just remains on the level of anecdote... seldom connecting the dots or seeing the developing tangents... One dot is not wisdom. You can prove anything you want from a single Scripture quote.'

* 'Some would think... the whole meaning of Christianity is to be able to decide who's going to heaven and who isn't. This is much more a search for control than it is a search for truth, love, or God.'

* 'Christians are usually sincere and well-intentioned people until you get to any real issues of ego, control/ power, money, pleasure and security. Then they tend to be pretty much like everybody else. We are often given a bogus version of the Gospel, some fast-food religion, without any deep transformation of the self; and the result has been the spiritual disaster of "Christian" countries that tend to be as consumer-oriented, proud, warlike, racist, class conscious, and

addictive as everybody else – and often more so, I'm afraid.'

* 'The people who know God well – mystics, hermits, prayerful people, those who risk everything to find God – always meet a lover, not a dictator.'

* 'If you were going to create a religion, who would think of creating as your religious image a naked, bleeding, wounded man? It is the most likely image for God; the most illogical image for Omnipotence.'

* 'Every time God forgives us, God is saying that God's own rules do not matter as much as the relationship that God wants to create with us.'

* 'The full and final Biblical message is restorative justice, but most of history has only been able to understand retributive justice. Now, I know you're probably thinking of many passages in the Old Testament that sure sound like serious retribution. And I can't deny there are numerous black and white, vengeful scriptures, which is precisely why we must recognise that all scriptures are not equally inspired or from the same level of consciousness.'

Wikipedia summarises the emphases in his writings and teaching: 'Scripture as liberation, the integration of action and contemplation, incarnation mysticism, community building, peace and social justice issues, male spirituality, the Enneagram, and eco-spirituality.'

Richard Rohr was born in Kansas, joined the Franciscans in 1961, and was ordained priest in 1970. He has a master's in theology (1970, University of Dayton). Richard has authored more than thirty books. He writes for *Sojourners*, the *Huffington Post,* etc., has been interviewed on the Oprah Winfrey and NPR shows and was one of the spiritual leaders featured in the 2006 documentary film *ONE: The Movie*. He has participated in media presentations with luminaries such as Rob Bell, Joan Chittister, Shane Claiborne, Laurence Freeman, Thomas Keating, Jim Wallis and the Dalai Lama.

If we must engage in 'hardening of the categories', let's put him with the people in his *Annotated Bibliographies*: like James Alison, Marcus Borg, Walter Brueggemann, Rene Girard, Gerald May, Eugene Peterson ('*The Message* is one of the most brilliant scholarly paraphrasing of the Scriptures I have ever read'), E. F. Schumacher, Eckhart Tolle, Alan Watts, Ken Wilber... (Theologically he describes himself as occupying a place 'on the edge of the inside'.)

The best place to start exploring Richard's wisdom is not, however, to put him into a theological box or category (he despises terms such as 'liberal', 'progressive', 'conservative', 'fundamentalist'). Start – with all mystics – with his wisdom on love. Like these:

LOVE

* 'As long as your ego is in charge, you will demand a retributive God; you'll insist that hell is necessary. But if you have been transformed

by love, hell will no longer make sense to you because you know that God has always loved you in your sinfulness.'

* 'It is not that if I am moral, then I will be loved by God, but rather I must first come to experience God's love, and then I will – almost naturally – be moral.'

* All we can do is fall into the Eternal Mercy, where we fall into a net out of which we cannot fall.'

* 'Love is the true goal, but faith is the process of getting there, and hope is the willingness to live without resolution or closure.'

I first 'met' Richard in the 1980s via his teaching cassettes when he was the charismatic (in both senses) leader of the New Jerusalem Community in Cincinnati, Ohio.

He currently serves as Founding Director and Academic Dean of the Living School for Action and Contemplation (CAC) in Albuquerque, New Mexico. The CAC's curriculum has seven themes, addressed in his excellent daily prayer resource *Yes, And...* **[2013] which is the culmination of Richard's life-long 'yes, and...' non-dualistic way of seeing all reality. He aims to avoid dichotomies, unifying what is usually divided** – the sacred and profane, natural and unnatural, contemplation and activism, life and death, orthodoxy and orthopraxy, prophetic and priestly, faith-plus-reason-plus-experience...

Yes, And... **features 366 meditations, each written by Rohr and adapted or excerpted from his many written and**

recorded works. It's an excellent daily prayer resource for those who are looking for an alternate way to live out their faith – a way centred in the open-minded search for spiritual relevance of a transforming nature.

The meditations are arranged around seven themes:

* Methodology: Scripture as validated by experience, and experience as validated by tradition, are good scales for one's spiritual worldview.

* Foundation: If God is Trinity and Jesus is the face of God, then we live in a benevolent universe.

* Frame: There is only one Reality. Any distinction between natural and supernatural, sacred and profane is a bogus one.

* Ecumenism: Everything belongs and no one needs to be scapegoated or excluded. Evil and illusion must be named truthfully: they die in exposure to the light.

* Transformation: The separate self is the problem, whereas most religion makes the 'shadow self' the problem. This leads to denial, pretending, and projecting instead of the real transformation into the Divine.

* Process: The path of descent is the path of transformation. Darkness, failure, relapse, death, and roundedness are our key teachers, rather than ideas or doctrines.

* Goal: Reality is paradoxical and complementary. Non-dual thinking is the highest level of consciousness. Divine union, not private perfection, is the goal of religion.

One reviewer's wise summary: 'This book of meditations may have the chance at transformation, not because it gives instructions on what to do or how to change, but because it helps us see reality differently... Read this book and you will find in Richard Rohr a spiritual director, a well of wisdom, a sacred companion, and a vision that will help you see not only what could be, but already is. Enjoy the journey.' [1]

ooOoo

One of his most strategic ministries is the international movement he founded focusing on encouraging men towards greater spiritual consciousness - Men As Learners & Elders (M.A.L.E.s). At one of his men's retreats in Arizona I vividly recall standing with the other guys in a circle, and each of us had to shout out to the group the main 'put-down' which came to mind from an authority-figure back in our childhood. Mine: 'Rowland, you're a nuisance, asking all those questions!' Then we started again, each of us shouting the same words: 'I'm a loved son of God!' There were tears everywhere...

I asked Richard if we could have a private lunch. 'Of course', he responded. His first question: 'Rowland, you're not doing this to get me to Australia, are you?' Moi: 'Who me? That's up to God and you!' It was 8 April 2005 and we talked about Pope John Paul 2 (whose funeral/Requiem Mass was being held as we spoke: it set world records both for attendance and number of heads of state present at a funeral). Verdict: 'Good man in many respects, but unfortunately, he was a bully.'

Soon afterwards, Richard did come DownUnder - then maybe eight or ten times more... I remember him telling a packed audience in Melbourne's Pharmacy College auditorium: 'Say Yahweh: breathe in, breathe out with each word-utterance.' And to a conference in Canberra, in response to a question about his gift-with-words: 'I did not ask for that gift: words just seem to form naturally as I speak.' And somewhere else (this is also in many of his books): 'I need a major humiliation every day.'

I remember a few years later talking with a 'fan' of Richard's in our guest room. 'He slept in this room', I said. The man – a converted 'biker' and well-read theologically – got up from his chair and laid his hands reverently on the bed...

ooOoo

Back to quotable quotes. Here are some I marked in a recent re-reading of *Things Hidden: Scripture as Spirituality* (where he cites Old and New Testament passages on almost every page).

* 'Most religion [operates on the] assumption that if you pass some sort kind of cosmic SAT test [and] get the right answers, God will like you.'

* 'Suffering of some sort seems to be the only thing strong enough to destabilise our arrogance and our ignorance. I would define suffering very simply as "whenever you are not in control".'

* 'All of the Bible is trying to illustrate through various stories humanity's objective unity with God.'

* 'The minds of saints and mystics... tend to be non-dual. They see wholes instead of parts.'

* 'Jesus is "once and for all", saying blood sacrifice is over, as René Girard pointed out so well in *Violence and the Sacred*.'

* 'If you are not trained in a trust of mystery and some degree of tolerance for ambiguity, frankly you will not proceed very far on the spiritual journey.'

* 'It is painful but necessary to be critical of your own system, whatever it is. [That] will never make you popular. The prophets are always rejected by their own (see Luke 12:50-51) and eventually killed.'

* 'Immature religion creates a high degree of "cognitively rigid" people or very hateful and attacking people – and often both.'

* 'Without a significant other who is also The Significant Other, we are burdened with being our own centre and circumference.'

* 'Jesus defines truth as personal rather than conceptual... [rearranging] the world of religion from arguments over ideas and concepts into a world of encounter, relationship and presence... That changes everything.'

* 'Saint Bonaventure, scholar and intellectual, said that a cleaning person can know God much better than can a doctor in theology.'

* 'A true Christian is invariably someone who has met a true Christian.'

* 'Torah, or Law, is the best and most helpful place to begin, but not the place to stay, and surely not the place to end. "Written letters bring death, but the Spirit alone brings life" as Paul said (2 Corinthians 3:6).'

* 'A prime idea of the Bible is its very straightforward critique of power, from Genesis to Revelation. For examples of good authority, see Joseph, Moses and Jesus; for bad authority, see almost everybody else!'

FINALLY, if all that's nice theory, how do we get to practise such love day by day? I can't think of a better 'how to' summary than Richard Rohr offered in an interview with Roland Ashby, editor of *The Melbourne Anglican* in December 2006:

> 'One of the particularly beautiful and memorable sentences in Richard Rohr's latest book *Contemplation in Action* is, **"We are all partial images slowly coming into focus to the degree we allow and filter the light and the love of God."** How, I asked him, can we begin to "allow and filter" God's light and love?'

> Richard's response: 'The key to this for me is what I call the contemplative stance, by which I mean

trying to live in a constant state of consciousness of union with God. Daily silent periods of prayer and meditation are an important way of developing this consciousness – and in my own life I also try to protect big chunks of solitude and silence, working in the garden and working silently in the house – but the goal of contemplation is to maintain this consciousness whatever you're doing, whether you're at work, with other people or on your own.'

Endnote

[1]   *The Englewood Review of Books*, November 2013.

Chapter 11
GROWING OLD GRACEFULLY

Headlines 2018 all over the world: 'Stunning anti-ageing breakthrough could see humans live to 150 and regenerate organs by 2020 for the price of a coffee a day.'

- A new technique could see the aging process in humans reduced by 50 years

- Researchers from Sydney found mice given the pill lived ten per cent longer

- The molecule could also regenerate certain organs by reprogramming their cells

- The drug could be available to the public in five years following human testing.

The science behind the new technique involves the molecule nicotinamide adenine dinucleotide (NAD), which plays a role in generating energy in the human body. The chemical is already used as a supplement for treating Parkinson's disease and fighting jet lag.

Professor David Sinclair, who is using his own molecule to reduce the ageing process, said his biological age has dropped by 24 years after taking the pill.

He said his father, 79, has been white water rafting and backpacking after starting using the molecule a year-and-a-half previously.

The professor also said his sister-in-law was now fertile again after taking the treatment, despite having started to transition into menopause in her 40s.

A breakthrough by Australian scientists could result in ageing bodies being reprogrammed to feel 50 years younger.

Researchers led by the University of NSW and Harvard Professor David Sinclair have developed a cell reprogramming process that could regenerate the human body. Professor Sinclair says this could help people live to the age of 150.

He said, 'We have discovered genes that reprogram cells to be young again. That is really on the cutting edge - we would not be just feeling young but actually being young again'.[1], [2]

ooOoo

Famous quotes about old age

- 'Growing old is like being increasingly penalised for a crime you haven't committed' (Anthony Powell).

- 'To me, old age is always 15 years older than I am' (Bernard Baruch).

- 'Most of us never get too old to learn some new way of being stupid' (Anon).

- 'Getting along in years is what happens when you know all the answers, but nobody asks you the question' (Anon).

- Old age, laments a character in Shakespeare, is 'mere oblivion, sans teeth, sans eyes, sans taste, sans everything'.

- Robert Browning was more optimistic: 'Grow old along with me! The best is yet to be; the last of life, for which the first was made.'

* Eugene Peterson's translation of Psalm 90:10 is interesting: 'We live for seventy years or so (with luck we might make it to eighty). And what do we have to show for it? Trouble. Toil and trouble and a marker in the graveyard.'

ooOoo

Each of us grows older every minute, every day. We – all of us – are 'the ageing'. Old age is, without question, one of the most challenging of life's stages of growth and development. If you ask people the benefits of getting older, often they won't be able to list any.

(Actually 'growing old' is a contradiction in terms: you really can't grow old; you can only grow new!)

As I write, I'm happy to declare that I'm approaching 83 years of age next December (2020). I've loved every aspect of my seniors' experience, except for one thing: my wife Jan passed away on 1 August 2017 at the age of 80-plus-two-months. So we both added a decade to the biblically promised 'threescore years and ten'.

Until recently, only a minority of the world's peoples have been privileged to live a long life. Throughout history, the elderly have had either a precarious or an honoured position in society. Hunters and gatherers who move around find that being old can be a burden. Eskimos sometimes left them behind when they could no longer care for themselves. The elderly among some South Pacific peoples sometimes paddled away into the ocean and died. [3]

ooOoo

Ageing is not always fun. As writer John Updike puts it – typically via his trademark eroticisms – in his 61st book, *The Widows of Eastwick*, 'It was in bed she first felt his death coming... In his body upon hers there was a palpable loosening in the knit of his sinews'. His novel doesn't reach the depth of other fiction about ageing, like Tolstoy's *Death of Ivan Ilych* or Philip Roth's *Everyman* but in his typically colourful fashion he writes about the sadness of the widows bumbling through Eastwick, being reminded by the locals of their past sins... [4]

So yes, ageing has a mixed press. My hernia doesn't allow me to walk fast or lift heavy stuff. (I should have known that when I sorted concrete pavers and my body duly protested.) When you Google Old Age, hundreds of jokes hit you first off (like Woody Allen's famous line about 'I don't mind dying: I just don't want to be there when it happens').

But here we'll look at a potpourri list of some of the classical and biblical wisdom about coping with - even enjoying - our senior years.

(1) **Signs of 'ageing'**: Here's a corny list I read in one of my files: You keep repeating yourself; you discover bifocals are stylish; when you do the 'Hokey Pokey' you put your left hip out and it stays out; you discover the words 'whippersnapper', 'scallywag' and 'by crikey' creeping into your vocabulary; you enjoy hearing about other people's medical adventures/ operations; you participate in heated discussions about the pros and cons of pension plans, retirement villages, etc.; you have more 'problem hair' in your nose and ears than on your head; you keep repeating yourself; you keep repeating yourself; you quit trying to hold your stomach in, no matter who walks into the room; relatives smile rather than interrupt you as you retell the same story for the zillionth time; you run out of breath walking down a flight of stairs; you sing along with the elevator music; neighbours borrow your tools; you are proud of your push lawn-mower; your arms are almost too short to read the newspaper; you keep repeating yourself; your relatives longingly refer to your things as your 'estate'; people don't harass you any more when you take an afternoon nap; despite your serious physical complaints, we can describe ourselves in terms like Mrs Malaprop's - an 'octogeranium'...

(2) **Seriously**: Others need the wisdom and experience the elderly can pass on to them. Others can learn from us 'oldies' about patience, endurance, the dignity of work, surviving in hard times, living with handicaps and, perhaps, pain, the value of nostalgia, and also about the secret of being a growing person even though our bodies are getting older and more frail. I just read again the apostle Paul's tremendous statement

(in 2 Corinthians 4:16): 'For this reason we never become discouraged. Even though our physical being is gradually decaying, yet our spiritual being is renewed day after day'.

(3) **The bad news**: Unfortunately, some senior citizens – in all the world's cultures – just sit about whiling away their days until they die. They're often confused by a changing world. Many customs they have been used to disappear, and new ways of doing things replace them... But those who habitually hark back to the 'good old days', and think and talk about how old they are, and the things they can no longer do, are old whether they are 40 or 90.

(4) **Intimate friendships are still important**. Oscar Wilde reckoned that 'other people are quite dreadful; the only possible society is oneself'. Wrong, Oscar, and sad. (There is more – negative – wisdom in something else he said: 'In this world there are only two tragedies. One is not getting what one wants, and the other is getting it'.) More positively, from a happy oldie: 'Growing older is a breeze. I don't have to do nuthin'. It just happens. Sure, there are negative aspects, like aches and pains, but that even helps my social life. We hurt all over, so the subject matter is endless.'

(5) **Geriatric psychiatrist Charles Wells M.D.** wrote a book *Dear Old Man: Letters to Myself on Growing Old* comprising letters to himself as he approached 60, about the values of a good life. Sample: 'We can and must learn to be more temperate, more courteous, more forgiving... So take advantage of your age. Tell yourself that you really have no

reason to do all those things that have grown unimportant to you. Take time to enjoy the freedom of old age'.

(6) Keep a schedule – even in retirement. It should be regular, but not rigid. Have a regular time of meditation/devotion, and a regular place to pray (it's called an 'oratory'). For many older people, the 'ministry of the prayer list' – intercession – is a valued one.

(7) **More from the Bible**: 'Grey hair is a crown of glory; it is gained in a righteous life' (Proverbs 16:31). [5]

(8) **It's never too late to start exercising your brain.** Michael Valenzuela, a clinical neuroscience research fellow at the University of NSW school of psychiatry – who won the 2006 Eureka Prize for his research into how maintaining an active mind can ward off the onset of dementia – studied 29,000 people and found that a lifetime of complex mental activity almost halved the risk of dementia. He says that even past middle age, there are still benefits from keeping the brain clicking. And it's better if you do it with other people, mixing hobby-friendships (like gardening), physical activities (join a walking club), reading, crosswords, etc. [6]

(9) **Tips for healthy ageing** produced by the National Institute on Ageing, USA: eat a balanced diet; exercise regularly: walking and swimming are best; get regular medical checkups; don't smoke: it is never too late to quit; practise safety habits at home to prevent falls and fractures. Always wear your seatbelt when traveling by car; maintain contacts with your family and friends, and stay active through work,

recreation, and community; avoid over-exposure to the sun and the cold; if you drink, moderation is the key; keep personal and financial records in order to simplify budgeting and investing; plan long term housing and financial needs; keep a positive attitude toward life; do things that make you happy. [7]

(10) **Sleep well** (I'm now speaking to myself!): 'Sleep patterns do change as we grow older, however sleep that is disturbed and unrefreshing is not an inevitable part of ageing. The amount of sleep a person needs varies widely between individuals. Getting a good night's sleep can have a huge impact on quality of life.

Tips for a good night's sleep:

- develop a bedtime routine and go to bed at the same time each night;
- try to get exposure to natural light each afternoon;
- avoid caffeinated drinks late in the day;
- don't drink alcohol or smoke to help you sleep – alcohol can make it harder to stay asleep, and nicotine is a stimulant;
- create a safe and comfortable sleeping environment;
- try not to worry about your sleep. If you find that disturbed sleep is frequently leaving you so tired that you cannot function normally during the day, please consult your doctor. [8]

(11) **Live in the present** as well as enjoying memories of the past. 'It is when a person begins to live (only) in the past, the good old days, that the boat begins to drift downstream, eventually coming to rest in stagnant waters' (Frank Case).

(12) **Serve others.** Some community groups and churches have an 'Adopt a Grandmother' program: connecting an older person who misses the company of children and a younger parent who has too much 'on their plate'. [9]

>Age is a quality of mind
>If you have left your dreams behind,
>If hope is cold,
>If you no longer look ahead,
>If your ambition's fires are dead,
>Then you are old.
>But if from life you take the best;
>If in life you keep the zest;
>If love you hold,
>No matter how the years go by,
>No matter how the birthdays fly,
>You are not old. [10]

(13) **Think about death and dying** (but don't get preoccupied with it!). A church ran a series of workshops: 'Having My Say for the End of My Stay'. They explored how best to begin the preparation and planning for the medical and physical realities of the 'death event' we will all inevitably experience. Let us embrace death not as an enemy to be resented and feared, but as a natural part of the ebb and flow of our multi-dimensional existence.

Growing old has nothing to do with the number of years you have lived. I am only as old as my despair and as young as my faith.

Someone said to me: 'Don't ever grow up!' My response, 'Hey, I'm too old to grow up!'

ooOoo

COUNTDOWN TO RETIREMENT

I gave an address to a 'Preparing for Retirement' seminar nearly two decades ago. (See the five articles written for The International Year of the Older Person on jmm.org.au for the substance of what I said.) As part of the talk, I listed all the reasons why I was happy to be over 60. (I've just moved some of the tenses to the present: twenty years later. Why don't you make a list describing your feelings about growing older?)

* These days I can sit and look at the trees and the birds without thinking I should be 'doing' something. I can relax with a clear conscience.
* I've achieved most of my life goals.
* Although we had a $90,000 mortgage my wife Jan and I for the first time in our lives were saving a little.
* Our sex life was sorted out.
* I don't mind doing a few chores.
* Jan and I knew 'who had the veto where' in our relationship. She had veto power in the kitchen, and

anything to do with colour schemes for house or car; I've forgotten where my veto lay!

* Our grandchildren were (and are) a joy; it's good that they're someone else's immediate/ultimate responsibility.

* I don't need recognition anymore (I sometimes switch off during fulsome introductions); I've nothing to prove anymore (which is one reason I mostly don't bother answering rude Internet Newsgroup - these days Facebook - posters).

* I have time to pray and read (including a few interesting and even inconsequential books).

* I've tried to learn a new skill every year: mastering a few corners of the 'Net has occupied recent years!

* Ours is a five-minutes-a-month garden (euphemistically called an 'Australian native garden'); I enjoy that.

* I've found myself enjoying talking to strangers for the first time in my life; most years I've been 'peopled out'.

* It's nice to be home most nights.

* I don't have so many 'accidents' or make so many mistakes (that I'm aware of).

* It's nice to be on one committee only: our John Mark Ministries Board, which meets about three times a year. (Update: some members of that Board have died

or retired: for others I occasionally check in with an emailed update.)

* I know my limitations (I think).
* I think I know how the 'demonic negativity' gets to me and how to thwart it (I'm still a Fundamentalist re belief in a creature called Satan).
* I don't worry about 'image' anymore; Jan often suggested what to wear.
* I can say/write what I think, and hopefully communicate with humour and love and wisdom; I don't need to score points against anyone anymore (unless they're part of an unjust system).
* I've realised that success will feed your ego, but never your soul.
* I think I know what can be changed and what can't.
* I toyed with setting a couple of new goals - like entering the Veterans' Olympics (I reckoned I could run faster than many of them!). (P.S. Gave that idea away: walking's just as healthy, and is easier!)
* I enjoyed beating my Freecell best-score with a 100-game winning streak. (If you don't know what Freecell is you're probably better off - more time for other things. OTOH if you want to chase it through the search engines, you'll find there's a Freecell game no one's figured out.)

* I'm now free to give more stuff away than I hoard, and I'm looking forward to the time when I'll know where everything – including books – is...

* I don't worry anymore about how slow the 'Net is downloading some sites; I just reach behind me to a pile of papers I can sort while it's happening. I have a conspiracy theory about the 'speed' motivation to buy the latest...

* Above all, I hope all the accumulated wisdom has equipped me better to do my job, which is to figure out how people, families and churches can be better put-together.

Finally, a biblical promise to encourage us as we grow older: 'Suffering produces endurance, and endurance produces character, and character produces hope, and hope does not disappoint us, because God's love has been poured into our hearts through the Holy Spirit that has been given to us'. (Romans 5:3-5).

Endnotes

[1] Also see the Epilogue, 'Dealing with Grief', in *Questions & Responses*, Volume 1, pp. 118ff.

[2] E.g., CHARLIE COË FOR DAILY MAIL AUSTRALIA, 2 September 2018 https://www.dailymail.co.uk/news/article-6121913/New-technique-humans-live-150-regrow-organs-price-coffee-day.html

[3] An Australian archaeologist may have debunked the myth that people in the Middle Ages did not live much past 40, by studying their teeth. Christine Cave, a scholar at the Australian National University (ANU), developed a new method for determining how old people were when they died, based on how worn their teeth were. And her research suggests many more people lived to a ripe old age in medieval times than previously thought. Over a five-year period, Ms Cave examined the teeth of more than 300 people buried in Anglo Saxon English cemeteries between 475 and 625 AD.

Ms Cave said existing techniques were limited in determining the exact age of older adults. She determined several were older than 75 when they died.

http://www.abc.net.au/news/2018-01-04/debunking-mythpeople-died-young-before-modern-medicine/9302356?utm_source=sfmc&utm_medium=email&utm_campaign=%3a8935&user_id=189a06c7c13f2f1ed-98948c535912b143b225129e6a851eee378c-c6dfefecb15&WT.tsrc=email&WT.mc_id=E-mail%7c%7c8935&utm_content=ABCNewsmail_topstories_articlelink

[4] John Updike, *The Widows of Eastwick*, Hamish Hamilton 2008. I've been reading Updike since his earlier books landed onto my Bachelor of Arts reading lists. His eroticisms can be a bit 'in your face' but his brilliantly racy writing style and humour are marvellous. (Items from *The Widows*: 'Without the sexual need to negotiate, there is little to curb neurotic crankiness'... And: 'Her wits had thickened along with her legs').

[5] See also Isaiah 46:4, Romans 5:3-5, Psalm 71:9, Leviticus 19:32, 1 Timothy 5:1.

[6] Richard Macey, 'Exercise the brain and forget dementia', *The Age* Newspaper

[7] Based on a printout by *National Ageing Research Institute Inc*. Parkville, Victoria

[8] Ibid., *National Ageing Research Institute Inc*.

[9] Rowland Croucher, *The Family: At Home in a Heartless World*, HarperCollins 1995, especially chapter 20, 'Grandparents Are Very Special People'

[10] Edward Tuck (1842-1938)

Discussion starters

1. Look up these Scriptures and discuss some of the opportunities and characteristics of the 'golden years' – and our response to 'elders' – they suggest. Proverbs 16:31, Isaiah 46:4, 1 Timothy 5:5-10, Acts 11: 36-43, Titus 2:13.

2. 'Do not cast me off in the time of old age; do not forsake me when my strength is spent' (Psalm 71:9). How can the young support old people more appropriately?

3. A chaplain to the elderly made this comment, 'The best thing we can do for the elderly is remotivation for good works.' What did the chaplain mean?

4. What can your church/community group do to mix people of different ages effectively together?

5. 'There's a difference between "caretaking" and "caregiving"... In caretaking, something is taken. In caregiving, something is given. And that something is love, warmth, energy.' In your experience, how does this apply to the care of older people?

6. The UN's 'International Plan of Action on Ageing' says 'Ageing is a lifelong process and should be recognised as such. Preparation of the entire population for the later stages of life should be an integral part of social policies and encompasses physical, psychological, cultural, religious, spiritual, economic, health and other factors...' How can your church/group help here?

7. There's an interesting German word *alterszorn*. It means the 'rage of age', and refers to the habit of some older people to go over the polemical edge. Why does that happen?

Chapter 12
MY HERO CALEB

How can one keep growing in faith, hope and humility – which produces serenity – into our 80s and 90s? Here's a sermon I've preached in many places.

I'm now in my 80s. As I reflect on those previous eight decades, I'm becoming more aware of the importance of several things that happened to me in my teenage years.

I grew up in a godly 'Plymouth Brethren' home in Oatley, a suburb of Sydney, Australia. My father and mother were very dedicated Christians, in a simple conservative Brethren kind of way. But I cannot recall a single meaningful conversation between my father and myself. However, I had a Sunday school teacher – George Clark – who actually took an initiative to get to know me. I would go around to his home Saturday afternoons, help with his gardening etc. We talked about many things, psychological and scientific and theological. And he taught me to drive his car.

One day we were on opposite sides of a small garden patch and he said something to me about me which profoundly changed my life: 'Rowland', he said, 'I reckon you're going to be very successful at whatever vocation God chooses for you'. I could take you today to the exact location in a backyard in Neville St, Oatley, where that unforgettable conversation took place. No one in all my life had ever said anything as encouraging as that to me. And it changed my whole life. Whether George's prediction eventuated is for other people to judge...

So I'm addressing these thoughts to young people - and to the 'middle-aged' and to the seniors here. (The rest of you can have a little nap!)

Our biblical hero/model is a guy about whom we know very little: Caleb, one of the two spies who brought a positive report about whether or not to enter their Promised Land. I've used variations of this talk to induct a pastor into a new parish ministry; a CEO of World Vision into his management role; and also an article for publication in the International Year of the Older Person, 1999.

What do we know about this man?

'Give me this mountain!' (See Joshua 14:6-13)

Caleb is one of my biblical heroes. We don't know very much about him, but the few clues we are given tell us of a very impressive man.

Caleb was a person who never stopped growing. His name – suggests one Bible scholar – means 'all heart'. He reminds us of John Bunyan's character Mr Greatheart.

M. Scott Peck's best-selling book about grace and maturity, *The Road Less Travelled,* begins, unforgettably, with the words 'Life is difficult'.

It is. Caleb knew that, but 'took life by the throat' and confronted difficulties head-on. At age 85, he came to Joshua asking for the personal allotment of land promised by Moses. He had a right to sit down and take it easy – take off his army boots and put on his slippers. He'd survived 40 years of wandering in the wilderness, and then the invasion of Canaan. Of the thousands who left Egypt, he and Joshua were the only ones the Lord allowed to cross the Jordan River into the Promised Land.

What do we know about this remarkably complete man that can help us understand how to live to a godly old age?

1. Caleb was a risk-taker for God; and he refused to be discouraged.

Caleb is a living example of the old adage 'If you can't beat 'em, join 'em.' Apparently the Israelites picked up various groups and clans as they journeyed towards their Promised Land – one of these was Caleb's.

He was a Kenizzite, an Edomite, which means he was a descendent of Esau rather than Jacob, and he and his clan became assimilated into the tribe of Judah.

Although this might seem opportunistic, don't forget Caleb would have had to live with the disapproval of his fellow-Edomites: 'What? Deserting us to join the enemy?' In times of war this is called 'treason', and Caleb and his clan would have had to be careful to watch their backs!

But despite his adverse pedigree, Caleb rose to a position of some prominence among the tribes of Israel. He refused to be 'a prisoner of his scripting'. In the Lord's work today, there is a desperate need for leaders like Caleb, particularly among Australians, who are sometimes not noted for nurturing 'tall poppies'.

Our Lord often made the point that God's fathering extended to all people everywhere. He bluntly targeted the narrow nationalism of his own people, particularly in stories like the good Samaritan where the (Samaritan) 'baddie' is a hero.

It's a wonderful parable underlining the necessity to love God through loving your neighbour – and one's neighbour is the person who needs help, whoever he or she may be. But note that love of neighbour is more than seeking their conversion, then adding a few acts of mercy to others in 'our group'. Jesus' other summary statements about the meaning of religion and life in Matthew 23:23 and Luke 11:42 involve justice too: attempting to right the wrongs my neighbour suffers.

'Ethnocentrism' is the glorification of my group. What often happens in practice is a kind of spiritual apartheid: I'll do my thing and you do yours – over there. Territoriality ('my place – keep out!') replaces hospitality ('my place – you're welcome!').

Sometimes, our non-acceptance of others' uniqueness has jealousy or feelings of inferiority at their root. You have probably heard the little doggerel, 'I hate the guys/that criticise/and minimise/the other guys/whose enterprise/has made them rise/above the guys/that criticise/and minimise…'

In our global village, we cannot avoid relating to 'different others'. Indeed, marriage is all about two different people forming a unity in spite of their differences. Those differences can of course be irritating – for example when a 'lark' marries an 'owl' (but the Creator made both to adorn his creation).

Even within yourself, there are diverse personalities. If you are a 'right brain' person, why not develop an interest in 'left brain' thinking?

The Lord reveals different aspects of truth to different branches of the church. What a pity, then, to make our part of the truth the whole truth. Martin Buber had the right idea when he said that the truth is not so much in human beings as between them. An author dedicated his book to 'Stephen... who agrees with me in nothing, but is my friend in everything'. Just as an orchestra needs every instrument, or a fruit salad is tastier with a great variety of fruits, so we are enriched through genuine *koinonia* with each other.

A Christian group matures when it recognises it may have something to learn from other groups. The essence of immaturity is not knowing that one doesn't know, and therefore being unteachable. No one denomination or church has a monopoly on the truth. How was God able to get along for 1500, 1600 or 1900 years without this or that church? Differences between denominations or congregations – or even within them – reflect the rich diversity and variety of the social, cultural and temperamental backgrounds from which those people come. But they also reflect the character of God whose grace is 'multi-coloured'.

If you belong to Christ and I belong to Christ, we belong to each other and we need each other. Nothing should divide us.

Snoopy was typing a manuscript, up on his kennel.

Charlie Brown: 'What are you doing, Snoopy?'

Snoopy: 'Writing a book about theology.'

Charlie Brown: 'Good grief. What's its title?'

Snoopy (thoughtfully): 'Have You Ever Considered You Might Be Wrong?'

This points up a central Christian dictum: God's truth is very much bigger than our little systems.

ooOoo

According to Deuteronomy 1:22, Moses was urging the people to go into the Promised Land and conquer it, claim it. Moses had told them over and over that God would be with them, and the land was good (see Exodus 3:8). But they did what many groups do who don't want to do anything – they set up a committee to investigate: let's send twelve spies into the land to search out the best route. Numbers 13 and 14 tell the story.

The person chosen – remarkably enough to represent the important tribe of Judah – was this Gentile Caleb. Joshua and Caleb and ten others explored a land 'flowing with milk and honey'. They brought back a bunch of grapes so huge it took two men to carry it. In the desert, they'd probably never seen grapes. In their wildest imagination, they hadn't conceived of grapes like these.

But there were two problems – giants, and the walled cities they lived in. So the committee was divided ten to two. Ten of the spies measured the giants against themselves: we can't do it, they said. They are stronger than we are. We're like grasshoppers compared to them. The spies had gone to Hebron, the very place where Abraham received the promise of the land of Canaan (Genesis 13:18). But all the promises of God to their great forefather, the power God had displayed so many miraculous times, were all forgotten as they saw those high walls and those giants.

Two – one of them Caleb – measured the giants against God. To a great God, those giants were very puny. Caleb was prepared to do what leaders are supposed to do – lead. But the people were restive, afraid of this mammoth new venture, and what followed is a good example of what happens when leaders let the crowd write the agenda. Fear degenerated into panic.

At this point, Caleb was a man in his prime, aged forty-five. 'Yeah, we can do it! Let's go! The Lord is with us – that's all that matters!' The trouble was the Israelites listened to the pessimists – and as a result spent 40 years wandering around the Sinai desert until a whole generation died off.

The problems, the obstacles, were huge but Caleb was the sort of person who saw problems as opportunities, difficulties as challenges.

One of the characteristics of 'statesmen/women' over other leaders is that they usually hold a minority opinion about something very important and have to wait until the tribes catch up. They are strong enough to be comfortable in the minority: if they believe their position is right, they'll stick to it, albeit showing patience and love to others who don't yet see reality their way. There's nothing much worse than the 'idolatry of the majority'.

The ten spies may have been perfectly accurate in their comparison: the people perhaps were like grasshoppers compared to the Canaanite giants.

There's no argument against being realistic. However, those Canaanites might also have been ordinary people whose size was magnified by cowardice and weakness. The size of the enemy is always relative.

Today, our secular culture seems a huge obstacle against the preaching of the Christian gospel. Australians are supposed to be unresponsive to the Christian gospel: we're reckoned to be about the most secular nation on earth; our public institutions less pervaded by religion than almost anywhere else. My belief is that Australians are very responsive when our message is both faithful to the biblical Good News and communicated appropriately within our culture. We've used excuses where we should have been more open to the wonderful opportunities all around us.

Where you stand determines what you see. Only half the facts will lead you to the wrong conclusion. Instead of comparing the giants with themselves, the ten spies should have compared them to God. The unbelief equation is simply 'facts without faith equals despair'.

So our task is to assess realistically the world in which we live, in the light of what God wants us to do in it. There are enemies – the world created by our sovereign Lord has been hijacked by an enemy, whom Jesus calls 'the evil one'. But there is milk and honey too. The creation mandate has never been revoked: God saw that creation was good: and if you see it with the eyes of faith, it's still good. Creation's sinfulness and fallenness is not its essence; goodness is. The Dominican scholar Matthew Fox has taught us that Western Christendom has for too long been infected with a Pharisaic mind-set: defining human reality primarily in terms of its sinfulness rather than the 'imago dei', our likeness to the Creator-God. Reminds me of the classic example of surrealist art: a painting emphasising the manure heap in the corner of the field, rather than the flowers all over it.

As a result of his faithfulness in bringing back a positive report, Moses promised Caleb a mountainous area near Hebron. Because of the negative recommendation of the other ten spies, Caleb with all the others was sentenced to '40 years hard labour' in the desert. But there was no hint that he was discouraged by that. He could have thrown up his hands in angry despair and adopted a 'What's the use, with this mob?' or 'I told you so' attitude, particularly when people started dropping dead all around him.

But all the great leaders in the Bible had their leadership skills honed in deserts (or, if not deserts, prisons). Neither Caleb nor we are exempt from that rule. Every leader has to find a desert somewhere for retreat and reflection and renewal.

And each of us gets disappointed in other people from time to time: they don't live up to our expectations. Joseph was sold into slavery by his brothers – but he didn't give up. Paul, writing with a sad heart, told how one of his friends had forsaken him to follow the world. However, Paul didn't cease preaching the gospel because Demas did. James says facing trials produces the ability to endure, the kind of patience that makes you perfect and complete, lacking nothing (James 1:3, 4).

And after all that, Caleb knew what he wanted: 'Give me this mountain'. He didn't ask for an easy job. It was the most hilly part in the area, infested by giants. Israel's enemies were strongest here – the most difficult part of the whole Promised Land to subdue.

But Caleb at 85 said, 'Give me that'. Caleb feared no foe and desired no rest.

There's a saying that a person of vision and faith does the most difficult thing now and leaves the impossible until later. That was Caleb. Let's get on with what God has called us to do and refuse to be discouraged. 'Let us not grow weary in doing what is right, for we will reap at harvest-time, if we do not give up' (Galatians 6:9).

2. Caleb was a man of faith and hope.

Fear looks at the problems; faith claims the opportunities. Sure there are problems. This life is not for the faint-hearted. The giants are big, their strength superhuman, their reputation terrifying. We're just like grasshoppers compared with the great tasks lying before us. How desperately we need more Calebs with their faith and courage and know-how to lead us into the Promised Land! And now forty years after the abortive spying mission, this giant of faith was still hanging in there. Despite the huge problems, Caleb plus God was a majority. When we understand God's faithfulness and power, the difficulties assume their true proportions.

Faith and hope (and love) are the keys to knowing God. There are two kinds of faith: *fides*, faith or belief that, and *fiducia*, faith in. Both kinds of faith are gifts from God, available to everyone (Ephesians 6:23, 2:8, 9).

Belief about God is necessary before we can have faith in God. So God is graciously revealed to us in nature, history, the prophets, the redeemed community, and supremely in

Jesus. When we read the Bible or hear the preacher and become convinced in our minds that this God is worth entrusting one's life to, we make the big commitment: we commit ourselves to God, with our hearts, our wills, our whole life.

Then we begin to nurture and exercise our faith to make it grow. The apostles asked Jesus to increase their faith (Luke 17:5). Jesus said 'Everything is possible to the one who has faith' (Mark 9:23). What we need is not so much great faith in God but faith in a great God! You don't have to have all the answers (like you don't have to know all about electricity before you switch on the light). Faith is trusting the Lord, even when we do not understand all that is happening to us.

But faith doesn't mean switching off your reason. In 18th century Europe, many churches had to make a fearful decision: should they install lightning rods or pray to God to protect them? Some opted for prayer, and attempted to appease the Almighty by ringing the church bells during thunderstorms (and 12 German bell-ringers died in a 33-year period). The congregation of the church of San Nazaro in Brescia, Italy, not only rejected the protection of lightning rods but also had sufficient faith in the sanctity of their church to store 100 tonnes of gunpowder in its vaults. In 1767, lightning struck the church and ignited the gunpowder, causing an explosion which destroyed one-sixth of the city and killed 3000 people. (Snake-handlers in rural America have died for similar silliness!) Jeremiah told his compatriots not to believe they were safe simply because 'this is the Lord's Temple, this is the Lord's Temple, this is the Lord's Temple' (Jeremiah 7:1-4).

But as our faith grows, and we know the God in whom we trust is loving, and utterly faithful, we sometimes have to trust God when our 'reason' can't supply all the answers.

Have you heard of the man who was mountain climbing in the American Rockies, along a very rugged track? Suddenly he slipped, falling over a cliff. He grabbed the roots of a tree and hung there. When he got his breath back, he looked down and saw an enormous drop. If he fell, he'd certainly be killed. Looking up, the cliff top was so far above him he couldn't climb back. In desperation, although he knew he was alone, he cried out 'Is anyone up there?' He was startled to hear a booming voice say 'Yes!' 'Can you help me?' 'Yes' came the response. 'What must I do?' The voice answered 'Let go!' There was a long pause, then finally the man called out 'Is anybody else up there?'

How does faith grow? A step at a time. In my files, there are about 200 stories of people who've had a strong faith. They all had these features in common:

Their faith grew because they had a particular view of God – a God who is always available, who loves us, who desires the best for us. So their faith is in a God who believes in us, as well as our believing in God!

This God is powerful, and is always trustworthy. So they fed their faith on the stories in the Bible, reading them over and over again: if God did it for them, God will do it for me!

- **They noted the importance of faith in the teachings of Jesus** (Matthew 8:10/Luke 7:9; Matthew 9:2/Mark 2:5/Luke 5:20; Matthew 9:29; Matthew 15:28; Mark 11:22; Luke 7:50; Luke 8:25/Mark 4:35-41/Matthew 8:23-27).

- **They used the faith they had, not the faith they didn't have.** And they were obedient in their use of that faith. In Luke 17, Jesus says we should forgive someone who sins against us seven times in one day! The disciples ask – reasonably enough we might think – for more faith to do this. Jesus brushes off the request, saying, in effect, 'What you need isn't more faith, but using the faith you already have! Your problem isn't faith or the lack of it, but obedience!' To grow stronger, you don't need a muscle transplant, but to exercise the muscles you have! Trust and obey says the old hymn – and that's still good advice.

- **They think of possibilities.** Just as Augustine wrote the biography of sin in four words: a thought, a form, a fascination, a fall, so faith begins with your thoughts of faith. Faith-full people 'image' possibilities, believing 'all things are possible to the one who believes'. They link their faith to a vision.

- **They verbalise this commitment to a dream** – they talk to themselves about it, and to others! They repeat faith-formulas in their prayer: 'I can do all things through Christ who strengthens me' (Philippians 4:13). 'Perfect love casts out fear' (1 John 4:18). (I'm sure you can find a few more texts!)

\# **But they aren't off-the-planet idealists**: they analyse situations; they research the whole thing; they get all the facts together; they find a need and fill it; they become consumed with this vision; they organise and plan to reach their God-inspired destiny.

\# **Once they've used their minds in all these ways, they are prepared to take risks** (the story of Abraham, leaving his secure home and country to ride off into the west appeals to them greatly!).

\# **They follow Paul's advice** in Philippians 4:8: 'Whatever is true, noble, right, pure, lovely and honourable... keep on thinking about these things'. Just as a clean engine gives more power, so a clean life is more in tune with the infinitely powerful God.

\# **They feed their faith by discipline and hard work.** Unfortunately, for many in our churches 'the faith' is a body of beliefs they affirm in the creed – 'faith about' God but not yet faith in God. The church is thus a social club with a religious flavour. It is very dangerous when such a church elects spiritually uncommitted people to high office. A church that's alive will be stretching their people's faith all the time.

The pastor of a dynamic church in England was preaching about the wonderful opportunities all around their parish. His text: Deuteronomy 1:19 ff. 'Look, there is the land. Go and occupy it as the Lord your God commanded. Do not hesitate or be afraid. The Lord your God will lead you.' To press his point he gave out 800 seedless grapes to the people (seedless in deference to the caretaker!). 'God is leading us!' he preached that day. 'Men and women of faith – lead, conquer, win – take these grapes to others!'

Hope - and optimism

Now 'fides' faith includes an ingredient of optimism, but biblical faith is more than optimism. So is the biblical idea of hope. The New Testament talks about the patience of hope'. Christian hope is deep; mere optimism may be shallow. Optimism may be a good natural trait – and have no religious connections at all.

'Hope', says John Macquarrie is his little book *The Humility of God*, 'is humble, trustful, vulnerable. Optimism is arrogant, brash, complacent... Our hope is not that in spite of everything we do, all will turn out for the best. Our hope is rather that God is with us and ahead of us, opening a way in which we can responsibly follow'.

Hope is not conditional upon trouble being removed. Hope means God is with us in trouble and in triumph. Resurrection hope means God is with us in life and death. Hope means the God who was with faithful people in the past will be with them always.

Hope is a primal human need. Victor Frankl was a young psychiatrist who had just begun his practice when the Germans took over his native Vienna and shipped him and his fellow-Jews off to a concentration camp. Then began the awesome task of survival. With his trained psychiatric eye, he noted that many prisoners simply crumpled under the pressure and eventually died. But some didn't, and Frankl made it his mission to get to know these special people and discover their secret. Without exception, those who survived had something to live for. One man had a retarded child back home he wanted to care for. Another was deeply in love with a girl he wanted to marry. Frankl himself aspired to be a writer, and was in the middle of his first manuscript when he was arrested: the drive to live and finish the book was very great. Frankl did survive, and has contributed greatly to our understanding of the human 'will to meaning'. He developed a process called 'logotherapy' which, expressed as a simple question, is: 'If the presence of purpose or meaning gives one the strength to carry on, how do we human beings get it touch with it?'

Caleb's answer was, in one word, HOPE. Human persons are 'hopeful beings'. Where there's hope there's life. That's because our God is a 'God of hope' (Romans 15:13); those who don't know God are 'without hope' (Ephesians 2:12).

Once, when Martin Luther was feeling depressed, his wife asked if he'd heard God had died. Luther replied angrily that she was blaspheming. She retorted that if God had indeed not died, what right had he to be despondent and without hope!

Hope, says Martin Buber, is 'imagining the real'. It is not fantasy or wishful thinking – like Mr Micawber's 'hoping that something will turn up'. It's not 'she'll be right mate'! Hope deals with imagining possibilities, then having the faith to work hard to see those possibilities realised.

3. Caleb was a man of energy and self-discipline.

'Faith' and 'hope' don't mean expecting God to do for you what you can do for yourself. As we said before, Caleb could have adopted the attitude 'Now I'm 85 I've earned the right to take it easy. I know Moses offered me that mountain country around Hebron, but how about switching to 'Plan B' – a nice fertile valley that's already been conquered so I can settle down?'

Caleb fought the great battle with the 'sons of Anak'. The story is described simply in a few verses in Joshua 15. Now I'm not suggesting you do this to people who oppose your goals: the kind of militarism that pervades the Old Testament must be viewed now through the prism of the more perfect revelation we have in Jesus.

We too have gigantic opportunities. Our task is to fulfil Jesus' mandate to care for the poor and liberate the oppressed (Luke 4:16-19) and obey his commission to disciple the nations (Matthew 28:18-20). Our task is to conscientise this lucky country, without diluting our Christianness as we communicate to pagans and the church Jesus' message of love, forgiveness, compassion and justice.

With God, the giants are vulnerable. Caleb was no fool, not blind or stupid. Fighting giants in mountain country is difficult. Fighting ordinary-sized people in mountain country is difficult when they don't want you invading their territory. (Ask the Russians and more recently the Americans - about Afghanistan!)

Note one more thing about Caleb. He wasn't part of the rebellion against the leadership of Moses and Aaron. There's no hint about a leadership struggle between himself and Joshua: he was willing to be accountable. He wasn't even elected second-in-command of the army when Moses died. But when he came to Joshua to claim his inheritance, they had the sort of relationship that led Joshua spontaneously to bless him. Isn't that nice?

Caleb's eulogy (Joshua 14:14): he 'faithfully obeyed the Lord' (GNB); he 'wholeheartedly followed the Lord' (NRSV); or as the *Jerusalem Bible* translates it he 'scrupulously obeyed the Lord'. I wonder if they'll say that about me, about you? Obedience means that when our Lord, our Master, our King asks us to do something, we jump to it!

So in the story of Caleb, you have, in contrast, the fear of people who look at difficulties, and the faith of those who look to the Lord. Just as he inherited the place where Abraham and Sarah, Isaac and Rebekah, Jacob and Leah were buried, may we follow in his footsteps.

It is a sobering thought that just ten people in the whole company of the people of Israel were able to infect the rest with their faithless unbelief. May God give us something of Caleb's strong faith hope and courage, so that we might fulfil our God-ordained destiny.

Let us get to know our God, get to know the world in which we serve our God, and let's get these two in proportion. With the help of Caleb's God who is our God, we can conquer these mountains. Let us go forward together in God's power, giving courage to those who go with us...

ooOoo

Congregational Prayer

Leader: Merciful God, we ask forgiveness
for whatever is wrong in our lives.
All: If we are causing unnecessary hurt, or treating someone
unfairly;
If we have knowingly broken a promise, or failed to keep a
trusted confidence;
If we have been dishonest, or conspired against someone for
our own advantage;
If jealousy is distorting our mind, or bitterness has hold on
our soul;
If principles, traditions, or possessions have become
more important than people.
Leader: In the name of Jesus our Saviour, help us own our
fault and seek our true self;
All: And return to the soul-place where we are free to seek
wholeness and change. Amen.

ooOoo

And finally, three prayers: for Senility, Serenity, and for Humility:

The Senility Prayer

God, Grant me the Senility to forget the people I never liked anyway, the good fortune to run into the ones that I do, and the eyesight to tell the difference. Amen.

The Serenity Prayer by Reinhold Niebuhr (1892-1971)

God, give us grace to accept with serenity the things that cannot be changed, courage to change the things that should be changed, and the wisdom to distinguish the one from the other.

And finally

A Catholic prayer for Humility

O God, who resists the proud, and gives grace to the humble: grant us the virtue of true humility, whereof your Only-begotten Son showed in himself a pattern for Your faithful; that we may never by our pride provoke Your anger, but rather by our meekness receive the riches of your grace. Amen.

...

Chapter 13
DEATH AND DYING

Three years ago, 1 August 2017, the beautiful lady I was in love with for 60 years passed away peacefully, in the local hospital.

She was 80 years old: 'threescore years and ten' plus a bonus ten years...

I and my three daughters had been with her on her last day.

The nurse said, about sunset-time: 'You can go and get some rest if you wish. We'll phone you if anything happens'.

A couple of hours later, we got the phone call: 'I think you'd better come'.

She had gone to a better place. She looked haggard but at peace.

We prayed together around her hospital bed. I stroked her hair gently and in my thoughts expressed a very, very deep sadness that the love of my life had departed, after four years battling an aggressive form of uterine cancer.

But I also rejoiced with her: she was now reunited with her deeply-loved mother. And with the little one – our first baby – who did not survive until his/her birthday and was born prematurely...

She lives in our loving thoughts...

And sometimes in our dreams. (One family member said to me the other day, 'I dreamt last night I was talking to her in heaven. She said "It's cold up here. Perhaps I came too soon".) Interesting...

Death+resurrection is the most certain experience that will happen to everyone of us...

ooOoo

I intend to live forever; so far, so good. (Unknown)

Death – the last sleep? No, it is the final awakening. (Walter Scott)

The song is ended, but the melody lingers on... (Irving Berlin)

Perhaps they are not stars but rather openings in Heaven where the love of our lost ones shines down to let us know they are happy. (Eskimo Legend)

As a well spent day brings happy sleep, so life well used brings happy death. (Leonardo DaVinci)

Say not in grief he is no more – but live in thankfulness that he was. (Hebrew Proverb)

People are like stained-glass windows. They sparkle and shine when the sun is out, but when the darkness sets in, their true beauty is revealed only if their light is from within. (Elizabeth Kubler-Ross)

> We make a living by what we get;
>
> we make a life by what we give. (Winston Churchill)

I can't think of a more wonderful thanksgiving for the life I have had than that everyone should be jolly at my funeral. (Admiral Lord Mountbatten)

> Yesterday is a memory, tomorrow is
> a mystery and today is a gift,
> which is why it is called the present.
> What the caterpillar perceives is the end
> to the butterfly is just the beginning.

Everything that has a beginning has an ending.
Make your peace with that and all will be well.
(Buddhist Saying)

More seriously:
My aim is to die young as late as possible.
I am determined to live each day till I die
rather than die a little each day that I live.
For me, life is a gift,
and the way to make the most of it
is to seek out the Giver
and to try to understand more and more
of the wonder of God's grace.
I will so live until I die and when I die, I will live.

Never be afraid to die;
be afraid rather that
when you reach the point of death,
you discover
that you have never really lived.
Llewellyn Handforth Evans (1913-2006)

I have regularly met sincere Christians who look forward – joyfully, not morbidly – to their dying... Their secret? Richard Rohr put it well: 'The people who know God well – the mystics, the hermits, the prayerful people, those who risk everything to find God – always meet a lover, not a dictator. God is never found to be an abusive father or a manipulative mother, but a lover who is more than we dared hope for.'

So, as the committed follower of Jesus Christ, St Paul put it (Philippians 1:21): 'For to me, living is Christ and dying is gain... and I do not know which I prefer. I am hard pressed between the two: my desire is to depart and be with Christ, for that is far better... [1]

ooOoo

I'm a pastor, so I've often conducted funerals. These gatherings are wonderful opportunities to convey sympathy – and hope – to the bereaved and their friends.

Searching my files, here are some excerpts from a randomly-selected eulogy/homily I offered for one of my parishioners:

'Today we say goodbye to a very special person, [name with-held].

'We come here with mixed emotions. In death – our own or others' – we collide with reality. There is shock, maybe sadness. There is fear and perhaps helplessness. Also deep appreciation, and gratefulness.

'Each response is OK: it's who you are. In terms of emotional experience there's no 'one size fits all'...

'But we're in the realm of mystery today. When death comes close, as it has in the loss of our dear friend/husband/dad/granddad, we are left struggling to find feelings that fit and thoughts that make sense...

'[He] had an eclectic range of interests: nature, photography, Christianity, classical music, and he even tried to teach himself Hebrew to broaden his understanding of the Bible.'

From one of the children: 'Mum and dad had a good marriage and as children we never heard a cross word between them. Any problems were discussed privately. Dad was a deep thinker but also had a cheeky sense of humour.'

'So as we commit... to the mercy of God today... Let us be grateful that our lives have been enriched by his life...

'[He] was a Christian, but not narrow-minded. For him death was not the last word; life is. Death is not the end of the human story; it's actually closer to the beginning. This for all of us is a temporary farewell.

'So back to our reactions today: God shares in our suffering and grief. The Lord knows the loss that we feel. Jesus himself cried with Mary and Martha when his friend and their brother Lazarus died.

'At the same time God gives a special hope in moments like these for "God is our refuge and our strength, a very present help in time of trouble". Jesus said, "Let not your heart be troubled, for you believe in God, then believe also in me."

'The Christian faith assures us that despite death life is not absurd and meaningless. In death, we are changed but life hasn't ended. In fact God has prepared a place for us that is infinitely better than where we now are.

'C. S. Lewis said it well: "I have never met a mere mortal"...

'Why is parting so painful? Because it is only when we have to part with people that we realise how much we love them. "Love knows not its own depth until the hour of separation" (Kahlil Gibran)...'

ooOoo

About thirty years ago, I wrote a book of 366 meditations called *Sunrise Sunset...* Just as sunrise and sunset are very special moments in the day, so birth and death are very special moments in the life of a human being. At these moments, we realise that each person is absolutely unique. At birth, something comes into being that never was before. At death, something passes away that will never be (on earth) again.

A Facebook friend composed a poem about death:

> Death, when it comes, will be such sweet release;
> To loose the grasp, let life slide idly by
> Into the depths of waters yet unplumbed
> And from all earthly pain and pleasure fly.
>
> Although for some, mere thought of their demise
> Fills them with dread in the encircling gloom,
> But no, not I! I'll gladly wrap the Reaper in his grim
>   embrace;
> For me no fear of grave or worm or tomb.
>
> You see, my life is hid within the One
> Who conquered death, broke mortal bonds of sin.
> Because He lives, my future is secured.
> Thanks be to God - I also live - in Him!

At the Thanksgiving Service mentioned earlier, we concluded the homily with an old Irish blessing:

> May the road rise to meet you,
> May the wind be always at your back
> May the sun shine warm on your face.
> Until we meet again, may God hold you in the palm of his hand. Amen.

ooOoo

Life is a mystery, not so much to be solved but to be lived.

We grieve against the backdrop of hope. Which is why despair is not part of all this for someone who follows Jesus Christ.

ooOoo

More wisdom from a Facebook friend: 'The average human being will live for 701,844 hours. You will be asleep for 233,600 of those hours (more if you're a cricket fan). You will be working for 74,060 hours (fewer if you're Usain Bolt) and you'll be waiting for your children to hurry up and get their shoes on for 11,850. Take off another 200,000 hours for miscellaneous activities such as being on hold for broadband customer service, queuing at the Coffee Shop, or looking up pictures of your ex-girlfriend's new boyfriend on Facebook...'

ooOoo

Funerals can be sad: like the one I did for a young man who put a gun into his mouth and sprayed the ceiling with his brains... How does one make sense of all that? He came from a family noted for its drunken violence: the sons used to swing their mother by the hair around the room...

But there are sometimes lighter moments: like the one where the organist played a beautiful rendition of Bach's "Sheep May Safely Graze" as the coffin was carried out of the church. After the service, the pastor complimented him on his performance. "Oh, by the way," the minister asked, "Do you know what the deceased did for a living?"

"No idea", said the organist as he began packing up.

The minister smiled. "He was a butcher."

ooOoo

What to do after someone dies

* An expected death at home is not urgent but a doctor needs to provide death certification.
* If the death happens in a hospital or care facility, staff will assist you.
* Grief support services can help you and your family with the loss of your family member or friend.
* There is support available for those affected by the suicide of another person.
* You may need to make decisions about organ and tissue donation.

* An autopsy may be requested for an unexpected death.
* An unexpected death must be reported to police and is dealt with by the coroner.
* A doctor must sign the death certificate before funeral arrangements can be made.
* The funeral director may register the death with Births, Deaths and Marriages.
* The funeral may be already organised and prepaid or you may have to organise it yourself.
* You must notify various organisations when someone has died.
* There may be financial issues that affect you that you need to deal with after a person has died.
* You are entitled to compassionate leave from work or school when someone from your immediate family or household dies.

What are people's top deathbed regrets?

Here's one hospice therapist's list:
1. I wish I'd had the courage to live a life true to myself, not the life other people expected of me.
2. I wish I had taken more time to be with my children when they were growing up.
3. I wish I had had the courage to express my feelings, without the fear of being rejected or unpopular.

4. I wish I had stayed in touch with friends and family.

5. I wish I had forgiven someone when I had the chance.

6. I wish I had told the people I loved the most how important they are to me.

7. I wish I had had more confidence and tried more things, instead of being afraid of looking like a fool.

8. I wish I had done more to make an impact in this world.

9. I wish I had experienced more, instead of settling for a boring life filled with routine, mediocrity and apathy.

10. I wish I had pursued my talents and gifts.

And finally:

'For I am persuaded, that neither death, nor life, nor angels, nor principalities, nor powers, nor things present, nor things to come, Nor height, nor depth, nor any other creature, shall be able to separate us from the love of God, which is in Christ Jesus our Lord' (Romans 8:38, 39)

'What the caterpillar perceives is the end, to the butterfly is just the beginning' (Anonymous)

'Grieve not, nor speak of me with tears, but laugh and talk of me as if I were beside you there' (Isla Paschal Richardson)

'Life is eternal; and love is immortal; and death is only a horizon; and a horizon is nothing save the limit of our sight' (Rossiter W. Raymond)

'Let not your hearts be troubled. Believe in God; believe also in me. In my Father's house are many rooms. If it were not so, would I have told you that I go to prepare a place for you? And if I go and prepare a place for you, I will come again and will take you to myself, that where I am you may be also.' (John 14:1-4)

Has this world been so kind to you that you should leave with regret? There are better things ahead than any we leave behind.' (C.S. Lewis)

Endnotes

[1] See also https://www.desiringgod.org/labs/to-die-is-gain

[2] Two good resources on death and dying:

Shannon L. Alder, author and therapist who had 17 years of experience working with hospice patients

https://www.betterhealth.vic.gov.au/health/servicesandsupport/what-to-do-after-someone-dies

[3] And some notes on suicide:

2,866 people died from suicide in Australia in 2016. The World Health Organisation reported the rate of suicide in Australia at 10.4 per 100,000 people per year (age standardised).

In the US, the number of people taking their lives has increased every year since 1999; a Newsweek cover story called it an epidemic. A study from West Virginia University found suicide had become the leading cause of 'injury death' in the US. 'In a time defined by ever more social progress and astounding innovation', wrote reporter Tony Dokoupil, 'we have never been more burdened by sadness or more consumed by self-harm'.

It's not just America; across the developed world, Dokoupil wrote, the leading cause of death for 15 to 49-year-olds was suicide – more than cancer, and more than heart disease: "Around the world, in 2010, self-harm took more lives than war, murder and natural disasters combined, stealing more than 36 million years of healthy life across all ages."

A few more notes about suicide

Many of us live lives of quiet desperation. (Thoreau) Dr Philip Nitzchke, Australia's noisiest euthanasia advocate, says hanging is the #1 method of suicide by old people. Nembutal is the poison of choice for those who want to euthanase themselves. More suicides than we might imagine involve head-on car crashes. Main complaint of old people? They're 'tired of life'.

1963 was a year (in Australia) with a suicide rate of 17.5 deaths for every 100,000 people, a level not reached since then. In 2016, the suicide rate in Australia was 11.7 deaths per 100,000 people, up from 10.6 per 100,000 people in 2007. [4]

In a week, 33 men and 11 women will kill themselves in Australia. We will not hear their names, the wails of their families, the guilt and sadness of those who would have stopped them if they could. Most will fall silently and not be endlessly dissected like the high-profile and prominent, the publicly adored.

Those at greatest risk are the young and the old, those in rural areas, those who have attempted it before, who have mental illnesses, drug or alcohol problems – or are male. In 2011, three-quarters of deaths from suicide were men. Young Aboriginal Torres Strait Islander men are 4.4 times more likely to suicide than other men of their age. Young Aboriginal women are 5.9 times more likely to self-harm than non-indigenous peers.

Causes?

The economy. High unemployment is a big risk factor, especially for young men. The suicide rate rocketed during the Great Depression and increased by about 15 per cent in the three months before, and six months after the 1987 market crash. Other research, cited by *Newsweek*, from Krysia Mossakowski, a sociologist at the University of Hawaii, found stretches of unemployment could permanently damage mental health: those who did not have jobs for long periods when young were more likely to be alcoholics, and depressed, when older.

Wealth and status. People with secure, high-paying jobs are less likely to self-harm. A study by Mary Daly, a researcher with the Federal Reserve Bank in San Francisco, found people who earned 10 per cent less than their neighbour were 4.5 per cent more likely to take their own lives. Which is sobering.

Availability of guns. In the US, half of all suicides involve guns. In 2010, the majority of gun deaths were people killing themselves, according to Pew Research. Federal Labor MP Andrew Leigh, when a professor of economics at ANU, conducted a study that found firearm homicide and suicide rates halved in Australia after the 1996 buyback of guns following the Port Arthur Massacre.

Media reports. An Australian Institute of Criminology report found: "The average daily rate of suicide in Australia increases significantly after the publication of suicide stories in the media". This is the contagion effect, which places the onus on journalists not to glamourise self-harm, or publicise details of the mechanics or specifics of suicide for fear of copycat effects. In an era of a flattened, web-driven journalism, this is, unfortunately, unlikely to continue to be broadly honoured. We need to be careful. But it does not mean we should not discuss or peel back the stigma of suicide.

A social safety net. The criminology institute concluded we have fared better than some European countries and Japan when it comes to self-harm, "largely due to the provision of a comprehensive social welfare system which has countered the vulnerability of high-risk groups to suicide".

Researchers have not been able to establish if use of antidepressants will curb self-harm; it is now recommended that psychosocial interventions be used as well.

It has been difficult to document the direct impact of national suicide prevention, mental health plans or substance abuse policies.

> [4] *Wikipedia*: Suicide in Australia (accessed 29 November 2018).

POSTSCRIPT

The aim of this series of *Questions & Responses*, is to address the 50 (or more!) 'ultimate issues' which provide conversations between my fellow Christian pastors, and their clienteles.

Feel free to email me (rcroucher@gmail.com) if you have any other suggestions.

The first three volumes addressed a number of core issues – but the remaining collections include some equally tough subjects, (and some biographical summaries of special people).

ABC'S OF EFFECTIVE PASTORAL LEADERSHIP
AFTER-LIFE: HEAVEN & HELL etc.
ATONEMENT
BAPTISTS (AND BAPTISM)
BELIEF-SYSTEMS AND CREEDS
BIBLE
BOOKS (Must-read-at-least-once-in-your-lifetime titles)
BRETHREN (And two people who've experienced them - Garrison Keillor and Brian McLaren)
CHARACTER issues
CHRISTIANITY: you decide!
COUNSELLING
COURAGE
CRIME
CULTURE (Musical tastes, etc)
DREAMS
DENOMINATIONS (Christian: 50,000 of them???)
EDUCATION

EMOTIONS (Like fear/guilt/shame/joy)
ENNEAGRAM (Know who you are)
ETHICS
EVA BURROWS (One of several 'best-put-together' women)
EVANGELICALS (President Trump likes them, and sometimes vice-versa)
EVIL
FAITH/DOUBT
FAMILIES
FREEDOM (Why is this issue so fraught?)
FORGIVING OTHERS (And yourself!)
FUNDAMENTALISMS
FUTURE: WHERE ARE WE HEADING?
GANDHI
GOD (What is God really like?)
GOOD & EVIL
HAPPINESS
HEALTH (Diet, exercise, sleep, etc.)
HEROES (Female & male, sacred & secular)
HOLY SPIRIT
HOPE
HUMOUR
INSTITUTIONS
INTERNATIONAL ISSUES
INTERNET
ISLAM
LEADERSHIP

MANHOOD/FATHERS
MARRIAGE
MEDITATION (Including 'Mindfulness')
MENTAL HEALTH & SUICIDE Issues
MIRACLES: REALLY?
MISSION (Be useful as well as decorative!)
MORALITY
MOTHERS
NIEBUHR (both Reinhold and Richard)
OTHERS/COMMUNITY
OUTSIDERS/MARGINALISED
PARABLES
PERSECUTION
POLITICS
POVERTY/REFUGEES
PRIDE and POWER
QUESTIONS (It's OK to change your mind)
RACISM
RATIONALISM & THE WORLD'S PROBLEMS
RELATIONSHIPS/FRIENDSHIPS
RELIGIONS (Are all religions equally true/helpful?)
SCIENCE
SECULAR HEROES (Mandela and others)
SELF-ESTEEM
SEX & ROMANCE
SEXUAL ABUSE
SIMPLICITY (The other side of complexity is best)
SIN (Especially the 'unpardonable' varieties)

SPIRITUALITY: Prayer, solitude, etc.
STRESS & BURNOUT
SUFFERING
TIME
TROUBLE
WAR
WISDOM
WORK
YOUTH

www.ingramcontent.com/pod-product-compliance
Lightning Source LLC
Chambersburg PA
CBHW070255010526
44107CB00056B/2469